"THE TELLINGS"

AND

"THE UNTELLINGS"

OF A WORLD SEEN THROUGH
THE EYES OF LIFE'S JOURNEY

J.J. ROBERTSON

ARCHWAY
PUBLISHING

Archway Publishing books may be ordered through booksellers or by contacting:

Archway Publishing
1663 Liberty Drive
Bloomington, IN 47403
www.archwaypublishing.com
844-669-3957

Because of the dynamic nature of the Internet, any web addresses or links contained in
this book may have changed since publication and may no longer be valid. The views
expressed in this work are solely those of the author and do not necessarily reflect the views
of the publisher, and the publisher hereby disclaims any responsibility for them.

Any people depicted in stock imagery provided by Getty Images are models,
and such images are being used for illustrative purposes only.
Certain stock imagery © Getty Images.

ISBN: 978-1-4808-9862-2 (sc)
ISBN: 978-1-4808-9863-9 (e)

Library of Congress Control Number: 2020921455

Print information available on the last page.

Archway Publishing rev. date: 12/23/2020

Table of Contents

Continue...

The Tellings And The Untellings

Acknowledgements

R.J.D.	LINDA C.	E.A.P.
CAROL D.	NANCY R.	R.L.S.
ALLAN D.	DAVID	R.M.R.
LUKE G.	FRANK	M.W.D.
KATHY B.	DENNIS	E.M.L.

WITH GRATITUDE AND APPRECIATION...

...TO THE AUDIENCE OF READERS...

...AND TOO...ALL THE WRITERS...

SUBJECT MATTER WRITTEN: MANY THANKS,
PROPERY OF: J.R. BRIEFS   J.J.R.

THIS...MY SECOND BOOK, IS DEDICATED TO THE MEMORY:

...OF...NICHOLAS NOEL...

About The Book

The journeys one endures…of life, of love, of loss…the emotions unseen, yet felt…of grief, of anguish, of guilt…..and the ills felled by its pain, torment, and madness; are but a few of the topics broached and so written in "The Tellings And The Untellings."

Its graphic climates are depicted in sound bites…real, specific, and painfully personal. Presented in settings that are veritably colored and drawn of, in, and to; a myriad of various selective themes…*tunneling*…it's way through a series of *Tales and Odysseys*. Its ledgers are vivid as each line is glossed in poetry and prose…while being phrased and measured within a frame-work, perhaps acrimoniously…semi auto-biographical.

Notions so ascribed within "The Tellings And The Untellings" are seen threaded and spliced with impressions that may seduce suggestions…*uncomfortably provocative*… unto the darkest *aisles* and innermost *sanctums* of one's mind. Essay's and storylines have been written to intrigue, titillate, and promote given notice into acknowledging the many facets that are stayed held, conditioned, and entrenched, in the somewhat self-absorbing…sub-conscious mind of man.

Subject material written in…"The Tellings And The Untellings"…may reawaken past remembrances long held, long hidden, and or perhaps, long forgotten. Throughout these writings….a plethora of given insights have been ubiquitously encased within *a cadre of passages.* They may come to evoke an *"afterglow"* to some members of this audience of readers: the curious and the pleasure seekers; *of times unsaid*!

As such, many have indeed…at one time or another, succumbed unto the throes of darkness, horror, and despair. Between the lines and within the readings are these tale's told in…"The Tellings And The Untellings". It will therefore become known to one and all…

…You Are Not Alone…

Within every storied episode, and within each tale, each odyssey has been flavored with elements consistent in use of…"Poetic License"…allegorical and alliterative. So styled in verse sautéed by rhythmic rhyming, and in musings both metaphorical and anecdotal with its narrative's…and within its messagings.

Table of Contents

Continue...

Table of Contents

Continue...

Table of Contents

Of "The Untellings" Told   "The Tellings" Of The Soul

IN SECRET LIE

From The Private Written Files Of The J.R. Trove:

"THE TELLINGS"

Impressions In Essay-Diatribes In Tale-Truths In Beliefs

AND

In Lament Soliloquy Touched In Prose...Versed In Poetry

"THE UNTELLINGS"

OF A WORLD SEEN THROUGH THE EYES
OF LIFES JOURNEY

Category Number One

Beyond The Darkening: The Aisles Of Man's Despair

Never Leaving Us…are the shames etched in our fears
Brought to bear…by our behavior toward one another

Never Leaving Us…are the hopes, wishes, and prayers
That mankind will soon learn…how to love each other

Never Leaving Us…are mankind's chains that we bear
As we battle…through God's land…alone or together.

And…
      Never Leaving Us…
            Are the tangled webs we weave…

In our conflicts…of war…
      …In our conflicts of life…
           …In our conflicts of love…
               …In our conflicts of peace…!

The following themes lends presence to…
The "Telling And The Untelling" dreams…
In mirrors prism…of reflections unseen…
Of our pains…our guilt…and of our pleas.

Another Tombstone

As the 1940's… with its wars of the world…seemingly ending,
A new life…with its wars not yet known…was now beginning.

The 1950's made its entrance suggesting peace and innocence.
He; was being learned and taught of sin by the *Devil's Mistress*.

With the 1960's…came wars…protests…and…*counter-culture*…
And soon he became evil's preacher, torturer, and its *vulture*.

Came now the 1970's and wars with constant changing scenes.
And a young soldier's son witnessing death and loss of dreams.

By the 1980's, war was his obsession. He…its prize possession.
Yet he carried forth the traditions of work, family, and religion
Only to be pained time and again…in tragedy and devastation.

In the 1990's…yet another world of wars…much like the old…
Was making its name known…across the whole damn globe…
And death's toll began mounting again…abroad and at home.

The 2000's brought with it…a new decade of terror and fear,
As wars were seen erupting…here…there…and everywhere.
And a soldier's eyes began to tear…watching lives disappear.

For in the years since 2010…with wars never ceasing to end
Another soldier son had by…The God's Of War…been taken.

And another mother cries…and another family is torn inside
And another father endures the night, in his fight to survive.

…While…

Another World of War and Hate…keeps taking all our lives.

About the author: In requiem of the inevitable (death)…
                          Are the "*Telling*" lines voiced in verse
                          Opening a "*Paned Window*" into his life.

The Autumn Realm

Within the shadow of an onsetting darkness...in rags tethered and torn
Shackled and chained...to a life claimed...of years weathered and worn
Now alone...as he descends unto the last throes...of Life's Autumn Fall;
He takes pause...recalling his final written lines of prose...now poem'd...

...*"The Autumn Realm"*...

Having once sauntered in memories now vague of youthful days of old
He dines in unceremonial languish! Watchful in eyes since grown cold.

Shamed by life's refrains...of its *"Telling Pleasures* and its *Untold Pains"*
He has stayed endured...*Riding The Iron Rails*...aboard a train helmed...
Towards his final destination...into the abyss...of *"The Autumn Realm"*!

As he genuflects upon...*Life's Triumphant Pages*...of the lives he has led,
He is reminded not of the *Pleasures*...but rather...the *Pains* held instead
And of his *Written Chapters of Regret*...in words spoken, yet never said.

Though saddened with penitence...he remains scarred of a life enslaved
While heavy with burdens he has long held. He'll now carry to his grave.
As night erases each day...he still writhes unrelentless...with callous toll.
Knowing his name is called, as *"The Autumn Realm"* beckons him home.

Ah! In a moments while came a smile as he found no reason in apology
For a life bled in *"Agony and Ecstasy"* in quest to *Champion His Destiny!*

Thus he quietly began in soliloquy...in praise poignant...of life's imagery:

With suggestions of life's...*afflictions*...of its givings, and in its misgivings,
And of life's endeavours of *"Love's Labour Lost"* and missed opportunity
Stepping Stones were being learned...as life's lessons were being taught.
And *temperance* had been served! As judge and jury were held to court.

As he now travels into *"That Goodnight"* and beds himself to a final sleep
He is comforted with acceptance that the true tragedy of one's existence
Would be to never have known of the trials...tribulations...nor experience
"Of Life's Telling Pleasures and its *Untold Pains"* so earned for one's keep.

Without trepidation, he now passes onward through the gateways held...
For his invitation into the netherworld...known as...*"The Autumn Realm"*!

The Shallow Minds

Oh!…How we define and categorize with…"Eyes Of Indifference"…
Man's addiction to suppress and malign…"The Color Of Innocence"!

J.J.R.

With predilections against…race…gender…and…Religious Interests,
Afflicted by…"The Shallow Minds"…of their own crippling sickness;
Man lies blemished and diseased…in "The Seeds Of His Prejudice"!

In footprints of "Self Indulgence" man has paraded his dominance,
Sporting his attitudes of bias…in criticism…ripened with arrogance.

Ambivalent to "Rules of Regulation" and in "Matters of Discipline";
He prefers enlisting his religion to temper "The Human Condition"!

He petitions not "The Moral Highground" avenging man's empathy,
Nor "To Freedom Man's Rights"…cozened in a "Sanctuary Society".

Rather…he adds labels to identify…his very "Pilgrimage In Apathy"
As he classifies all that he sees: into "Life's Cubicles Of Bigotry"…!

Though man's walls and barricades…have had their time and place,
They need stand no longer…to intimidate…separate…or to debase;
The traits now beheld by man…emblazed by God's forgiving grace!

As man's history has now "Fathered In"…a new millennial century,
Let his "Moral Compass" be…the map to now course man's liberty.
And let his quest for "Rights Of Freedom" soon become his reality.
No longer shall he be the casualty to man's "Category Superiority"!

Let he no longer deny "The Rise Of The Meek Nor Of The Innocent."
And thus let…"The Shallow Minds"…of man's; self-afflicting illness…
Be entombed together…within…"The Seeds Of His Own Prejudice"!

Dead End

Am reviled by stained hallway's…bloodied through man's damnation
Am felled by poisoned walkway's…in disease of man's condemnation
Am sorrowed by darkened pathway's narrowed by man's indignation.

And as man flames the roadway's…with *"His Torch Of Devastation"*…
Signs of a life's fractured highway…has given *burn* to man's salvation!

In Course Of Discourse

As each sunset calmly descends…
         …against the wake of its sleeping night
And as each new sunrise ascends…
         …breathing fresh hope in its rays of light
Man continues his Reign of Wars…
         …as he rages on…"In Course Of Discourse"…
Disrupting the cycle of nature…
         …and of "God's Commandments of Laws"!

And while I stay paralyzed in pain…by the failings seen of mankind
Alone I am oft to lament…*in the stilled and the quiet of my mind…!*

Curious with wonder, concern, and disbelief…in awe I am each day
For I see too many have stayed satisfied…mired in their own decay.

Oh…how is it, *that mankind rathers to bleed*…than find their way!

And as I remain aghast as to why so many…
         …repeat their mistakes and move nowhere in time…

Alone I am left once again to lament…
         …In the stilled and the quiet…of my mind!

Of Mankind's Chains

Another thousand years...plagued by war and anarchy
    Another thousand years...in pain, in tears, in misery
        Another thousand years...of terror, fear, antipathy

Oh...Dear God! How uncivilized still...has civilized man come to be!

How much longer can man survive without change
    And how much longer shall he wear...his shame
        Carrying the weight..."Of Mankind's Chains"...

Is there not need for mankind...
    To adapt, to adjust, to assimilate
        To listen, to learn, to educate
            To accommodate, to acclimate

Is there not need for mankind...
    To provide shelter, and protection
        Without malice, nor pretention
            Without prejudice or deception

Is there not need for mankind...
    To reprimand racial discrimination
        To hold equal, without separation
            To voice civil, its moral obligation

Yes! There is a need for mankind...
    To condemn acts of bias and bigotry
        To stand for equality and liberty
            To give comfort, aid, and safety

Yes! There is a need for mankind...
    To exercise his sense and decency
        To elevate dignity and integrity
            To embrace peace...not hostility

Yes! Now is the time and the need...
    For humanity to begin turning the key
        In the unlocking "Of Mankind's Chains"
            Being Helled of evilry, hate, and greed!_

The Screams Of Silence

Into the quietness of the human mind…shall silence still scream!

J.J.R.

As the hours of his darkness…must come to its long nights end…
A guilted soul awaits…"The Screams Of Silence"…to begin again.

As the church bells ring aloud…before the dawn of a telling sun,
He rises from another restless sleep…and turns, to find no one.

As warm showery waters have begun to run a bit cold this day…
Dressing quickly, he pauses…Yet he see's no need for he to stay.

> Heard in the distance…are life's slow whispers
> And the sounds of nature…squirreling around.

> While outside his window…he hears the swirls,
> Of leaves rustling about…in its autumn ground.

And as the howling winds of October…have begun to sweep down
Heard are "The Screams Of Silence" being echoed in every sound!

Stepping into the memories of another room; there is no escape,
For atop an unlit stove…is yesterday's coffee cold, he now takes…
Before he "traffic's" through the tears…along his lonesome way…
Into the sounds of life's empty crowds…and into his lonely place!

As he arrives into the coldness of the air…with rosary held in hand,
He kneels to give praise and prayer…for the one's now lying there.
For in the stillness of time…it is of their screams that he must bear.
While haunting cries from beyond the grave he hears everywhere.

> As he returns to an empty house…once his home,
> He enters yet again, into another darkened night
> And beds himself, unto life's final sleep..all alone!

No longer shall…"The Screams Of Silence"…torment his very soul!

Category Number Two

The Appreciations...
    Love...Folly...Beauty...And...Dreams!

An "Untelling" love kept in one's heart above
A "Telling" heart...yearning for another's love.

A love's growing friendship...a love's glowing light
A love's appreciation found in one's heart tonight

Of love's cherished feelings...of love's heart and soul
Of the love once let go..of the love one longs to hold

Let dance in the mind...of love's both young and old:
Of the dreams....the promises...and of the wonders...

...Of it all!

Of such...are love and emotion so characterized within
The next selections...so poem'd.

Of A Heart Genuine

As a poem renders verse...resplendent of poetic picturesque beauty
And each sunrise encourages a new and bright awakened curiosity...
So too, has a kind solace entranced again in comfort and generosity.

Tis grown from this flower blossomed "Of A Heart Genuine"...is she.

For a shoulder to lean and an ear to listen
Friendships build as bonds are christened

Unbeknownst she breathes of a trust seldom seen in kind
Yes...she is this flower blossomed..."Of A Heart Genuine".

People gather and together all are charmed delightedly...
Fulfilled by her gracious givings...of warmth and sincerity
And a gallery now thrills with music, cheer, and harmony.

Infectious as children's laughter and of innocent smile
Her presence lets us table our troubles for just a while.

For those fortunate to be amidst this woman's company
All will agree she gives of her strength...oh so unselfishly.

Tis grown from this flower blossomed "Of A Heart Genuine"...is she.

As we're touched by these gifts that few possess
We are reminded of her unfettered selflessness
With concern for others, a quality so hard to find.

There exists...

...This flower that blossoms...

...*Of A Heart Genuine*

Love's Loss

A scented fragrance assailed…amidst the flowers and trees
Aroused within the garden, an aroma whispers in its breeze.

Feeling's of love's passions'…aflamed by that night of bliss
Am remembered of a first embrace…that soft summer kiss.

And for just that shortened while…time had stood ever-still!

Memories once sharp have now been dulled along life's way
And across that fragrant garden…I now sit alone on this day,
Flooded by emotions cried alive…of when she walked away.

And for just that shortened while…time had stood ever-still!

Of day's long ago, we had enjoyed our shared togetherness,
Having found a love divine…warm with heartfelt tenderness.

But as the years began to expand…the portfolios of our life
"Love's Loss"…lay plagued by its struggles…and to its strife.

Blinded by the pressures we faced…caged in the unknown,
In defiance of each other, we died fighting together…alone.

Too late now…for that scented garden has emptied its will,
And for just this shortened while…
                    …Time stands not…
                                …Ever-Still!

Of A Naked Youth

Of youthful exuberance through open fields of play
As I recall those dalliances that caught me that way.

Illuminous wintery nights…warmed by the fires flame
Blistering blinding love-making…no thought of shame.

In fields of pleasure…and in gardens bedded bouquets
No boundary existed…would ever dare keep me away.

Ah! Such was this fool who knew of love through-out
I remember…what those dalliances did embark about.

Enjoying perilous escapades of love and sinful bliss…
Eyes wide shut then…I know now of all I have missed.

Reflections of a golden time…in moments like this…
Gives life's passages meaning…to what love truly is!

…The Love I Lost…

Into her waiting arms…did she so clothed me with grace
Into her innocent eye's…did I find…love's soft…embrace

Through all of life's years…did we become one-together
Sharing our heart, our soul…and our love of one-another

Gone now and forever…for our time hath run its course…

I lament with fond remembrance's of…

…"The Love I Lost…"

The Life Significant

As an absence...of life's success
Wreaks havoc...on man's significance
So breathe he...the air of emptiness
Leading him into...despair and loneliness.

J.J.R.

Of man's quest...In his desiring of life's golden opportunities,
Take heed to its tender mercies...and to its spirited bounties.
For there is wealth in the bonds...so gifted by its generosities

Hold dear indeed...all your memories' moments...so received
And enjoy in the love's shared by both...friends and in family
Keep your eyes opened and mind alive...in all you see and do
Then take comfort in the treasures that life has awarded you

Frame forever...pictures captured with kindness and decency,
And in playground sounds...of children laughing so innocently
Accept the joys and sorrows...and the cycle's of life's realities
Then draw upon your belief...the calling of a higher authority.

Stand tall against man's injustices...and his vulgar obscenities
Engage with proper discretion...as you battle bias and bigotry
Spread understanding as you bring forth...honor and integrity
Then hold open your window bright...take in life's curiosities!

Welcome all with warmth...and an open heart
Then keep within you...life's beauty...life's art.

For it is in these principles...that one shall come to recognize
As to what gives meaning...worth and value...in a life realized

Be careful as to what you wish...as there is many a difference
In man's definitions of success...and in the learned interest...

In living..."The Life Significant"

In Question

Does a dream somehow…
Bring one peace in being…in seeing…in believing?

Or does a dream…feign surprises…
In disguise of fantasies…deceiving…unbelieving?

And why are its colorless threads…
…sewn with…
Fabric enmeshed in dreams masked by the …"ID"?

How can a dream…act to blindfold…
A mind's sleeping *subconscious soul*…
Of its *tellings*…unto the unknown?

Is a dream…"In Question"…of a tale to unfold,
That is born of the mind…Imagined in the soul

Do dreams speak of *untelling* secrets…it may hold,
To thus awaken the *conscious self*…of all it knows?

A Silhouette For a Dream

Of life's realities…there exists a realm of…"Lost Illusions"…unseen,
And of life's questions…there exists…"A Silhouette For A Dream"!

Perhaps we are given a life on Earth to live…maybe another to find,
Perhaps one to receive…furled in a "Quantum Dimension Of Time".

Perhaps we are ordained to compromise…"The Tenor's Of Reality."
Perhaps we are orchestrated to suspend "The Realms Of Ubiquity".

Perhaps we cannot face the answers to "Life's Existential Entities"!
Perhaps we'd rather stay steadfast…to the past lessons of history…
And stand in denial of the vast realms of…"Life's Celestial Destiny"!

However, to behold the masks of life's realities…you shall indeed…
Cross into the realm of…"Lost Illusions" that is seen and believed…

…In "A Silhouette For A Dream"!

<u>.....*Love's Lullaby*.....</u>

You didn't at first, make no mistake…enter my mind.
Sitting behind your desk…quietly busy…quite refined…
Hair propped, posture erect…and oh; that beguiling look.
As our eyes met…you smiled and spoke…that's all it took.

Together we sat and talked, you and I…for just a minute
In conversation, you knowingly …with mischievous wit…
Displayed about you…such an easy and splendid style,
I knew then…I had to stay for more than just a while.

How could it be…that you would so capture my heart
So young and delicate. So bright. Ah! So avant-garde.

Am I now…not this fool…this child again…
In chase…in want of love…and its torment.
Stop me from opening…yet another door…
Lord knows…I've opened…too many before.

Old and beaten am I…with no time left for bliss
Realizing that love can only be a dream…a wish;
And a heart knowing…that love…shall never be…
For the todays are you! The yesterdays were me!

I will see you again…and as our paths will cross
Love and loneliness…will both touch and torch…
My awakened desires…I had once thought lost.

Am I now…not this fool…this child again…
In chase…in want of love…and its torment.
Stop me from opening…yet another door…
Lord knows…I've opened…too many before.

Category Number Three

*Daggers:

The Hearbeats Of Life And Death*

Oh! But for…"The Sins Of The Fathers"…

…and for…"The Sins Of The Sons"!

As I am to bury my dead…

…and take care of the wounded

…I shall carry their pains of sin

…for it is in "His" footsteps

…that I now….Walk In.

In search…for inner strength…

…in sake of family…for sake of self

…in my attempt to feel

…in my attempt to heal.

Note:

The following are readings……of a heart still bleeding…

…of a man left standing… and of "The Tellings" seen…

…of the realities of life's "Untelling" tragedies…

…and of his unsung dreams!

In Mourn Of Strength

Today, as we both lay our child…
    …unto his "Final Resting Place".

Memories of our past wounds…
    …we buried, too…with quiet grace.

For together: we held strong…
    …in mourn for one last embrace.

With an inner strength needed for all to survive…
    …I now pray for "Thy Savior"…
    …to keep my family alive.

In sentiment of us and of our "Seed Of Time"…
    …"In Mourn Of Strength"…I lament in these lines…
    …"To The Ties That Bind"…"To The Life Intertwined"…

Yes, we've had some smiles to share
    Yes, we've had some dreams come true
      We've had our moments full with tears
        We've endured those sorrows and losses too.

Everlasting is our love…
    …Ever meaningful as before
      …Of kindled fires once stoked
        …A love grows evermore.

Know that if it weren't but for you…
    I know I would have never made it through!

The Awakening Soul

A "*Spirit*" within…has been grown pure and whole
    Placed beyond above…in "*God's Almighty Soul*".

"*Saviour*" that he is…ever so humble, ever so true
    He is at your side, fighting the evils…fighting you.

Pain and suffering have pierced thy heart tonight
    As dark truths lay in ashes of a life once lit bright.

In tests now given, as you face "*The Devil's Fight*"
    Let of "*The Christ*" in you…shine his "*Guiding Light*".

Bringing forth "*Angel's Of Conscience*" for you to see
    He is forever keeping you within his close company.

For "*Thy Lord*" has graced to thee…of ear's so to hear
    And has set unto thee…of eye's to see, ever so clear.

As your beliefs have held steadfast…in strength and faith
    You now hold of the "*Key*" to unlock "*Heaven's Gate*".

Know that his "*Interventions*"…hide's no mystery at all
    For I have been witness of…"*Thy Grace From Fall*"!

As these truth's unfold, so shall your heart be known…

…"Of The Awakening Soul"…

Almighty God has saved…for the one you so dearly hold!

The Gift Of Share

Of the struggles seen in our children who cannot get out of the cold
It is the "Share" of love and family that will bring them unto thy fold.

Of the people gathered today for prayer...
Let a love be given in "The Gift Of Share."

As we are being faced with saving these *"lost children of the night"*
Let all of our faiths be now graced in "Share"...to this lifelong fight.

Tonight many have found they are in "Share" in this common history
And though together we smile in courtesy, we tear inside...mercifully.

An unquelled silent emotion is now felt by all that have braved here...
As we listen and bear witness for those whom have come to "Share."

We give question as to what went wrong, and what we can now do...
As all cannot secret these pains nor the guilt we've all gone through.

For all here today who will soon leave, to walk-down that lonely avenue
This "Share" is not only of our children...but a "Healing" for me and you!

Today we remember from each, "The Share", The Touch, The Embrace...
And the unconditional love..."Shared"...by all within this gathering place.

For The Son Shall Also Rise

Every now and then there comes a moment in time when the trials of life's realities; its triumphs and its failures in defeat...may come to recognize the existence of each other's hidden demons. These internal conflicts that stay unseen, *yet so telling*, are borne from within. It is a frenetic ongoing battle imbued through the temptations of good versus evil. It is an inner constant fight to maintain composure and control and to relinquish and extinguish too, of the fires that have so stoked and so inflamed the *mind, the body, and the soul*, which is the very essence of the being that is you. Dear Son...now is your moment! You have been given reprieve for your contrition and for your repentance. You are now being accorded...through earnest conduct...to receive *heaven's elusive aura* that so brightens the avenue's leading the way forward, onto... *"The Road Of Opportunity."* Go now...proceed ahead as you carry life's precious gifts.

...For The Son Shall Also Rise...

Take with you thy *cleansed spirit* you now possess. Hone afresh and enhance anew, of those skills and talents that will soon befriend you. Venture onward unto a world that awaits. Go forth with inner strength, with deepened thought, and with purpose worthy of those precious gifts. For they are but a few of the *stepping stones* used in acknowledging, and understanding...the carriages involving life and its experiences...

...For The Son Shall Also Rise...

Such are the choices to contemplate while *shedding your skin* of old, as you begin to again...re-enter the wonders of a new world. The man you are to become, may now face...*life's cycle's of challenges*...with a newly-found conviction in belief, while your journey continues to travel beyond.

Compassion in, and of a heartfelt cause, will provide aid as you graduate further into the *throes of passion* that will beckon forth in *life's emotional roller-coaster ride*. For you my son will find within "The Tree's OF Life And Knowledge", that as one matures one also becomes aware of *the blessed values* that is nestled in the heart, cradled in the soul, and stays endured within the mind. You will be enlightened as to the many facets of love given, love needed, and of love's glowing warmth. And yes; of the love that is to be felt and shared.

With new frontiers to explore, to capture, to behold, in your *passages of life*...I shall slowly and comfortably recede in fatherly pride into life's *background*. You, my son, will come to gladly appreciate the glory of what life is, what love is, and what living in truth means as you find your *stand* in the realm of life's...Oh so curious mysteries!

...For The Son Shall Also Rise...

In Memory And Tribute

At What Price Freedom

Blessings bestowed for each and every woman and man...
That have courageously fought at sea, in air, and on land,
So that an America...may always have our freedom stand.

This honored nation...and its people...rise to salute you!

Of the sacrifices which all families have so had to make...
Losing loved one's in the struggles against evil and hate,
Yet carrying forward, despite the sorrow and heartache.

This honored nation...and its people...rise to salute you!

For all that soldiered forth...braving in battle: unselfishly,
Taking on "Enemies at the Gate", keeping alive humanity,
Giving hope for survival's freedom...and America's family.

This honored nation...and its people...rise to salute you!

Let now...The chimes of freedom...forever ring true!

Dedicated to Nicholas Noel..."In Memory And Tribute"...
And in his prayer for peace...and in his prayer for truth...

Category Number Four

Power And Fear

    Gifts Of God…Errors Of Man

The following three short subjects described…

Are one page storied poems sending messages

Of history…

     …With promises of hope...

For the good…

     …For the faithful…

And for…"The Red Lines Crossed In The Sand"!

1) *The Trials of God's Child*   PG = 22

2) *Perdition*   PG = 23

3) *After The Fall…Then The Rise* PG = 24

The Trials of God's Child...

In The 1ˢᵗ Beginning… as mankind was placed unto a world yet unknown
Upon an "Eden"…spruced betwixt a moss covered "Garden Of Stones"…
Laden in *Fruits-Ripe*…"The Tree's Of Knowledge And Life"…stood grown!

To "God's" chagrin man now sinned tasting "The Forbidden-Fruit" shown
Thus man's chosen volition "Raised God's Wrath"…to path his way alone.
And on "Hallow Ground"…Seeds of Ignorance and Innocence were sown!

Of A 2ⁿᵈ Delivering…as man be moiled by "God's Deluge"… upon his lands
"God" echoed to "Noah", a pious man…Revelations to begat in command
For atop a Peaked-Horizon shall Noah come to be…"The Father Of Man"!

Furious of the sins and evil spawned by man…A 3ʳᵈ Reckoning now began
As "God" Fire-Forged in stone on a "Sinai-Mount" above the desert sands
The Commandments for Moses, a holy man, to teach of "God's" demand.
And thus "The Exodus" sojourned on…in search for "The Promised Land"!

Ah! At the displeasure of "Our Lord"…A Final 4ᵗʰ Awakening had begun…
"Our Saviour Father" begot unto man…"Jesus Christ"…"God's Holy Son"!
And in sermons did "Jesus" preach…"God's"…spoken word for everyone.

Too late! For…"The Sins Of The Fathers"…and…"The Sins Of Their Sons",
Denied "God's" word…*"In Crimes Blasphemous"*…Deigned In Crucifixion
"God"…be not denied! In 3 days would arise…"Jesus In Resurrection"…!

Knowing of "Our Lord's" attempt to quell…the *Plagues* mankind beheld
Hath "God" not falter…*To Smite the Splinters*…of this man-made "Hell"?

The Jigsaw in the Puzzle?....*Man's failure to abide*….In The 1ˢᵗ Beginning!
For "God's" pieces to fit?…*Man doth be cleansed*…Of The 2ⁿᵈ Delivering!
Of man to recognize Sin?…*Thou shalt heed "God"*…In Thy 3ʳᵈ Reckoning!
For thou Jigsaw to end?..*Man is Reborn*…In "God's" Final 4ᵗʰ Awakening!

Though "God" is mysterious to some…"In God Will Thy Kingdom Come"!

Perdition

Heard are the cries of death… on mankinds march to "Perdition"
His hatred and unrest have been carved…in Blood and Prejudice
Unleashing God's wrath and the Seven Seals of The Apocalypse!

Denying God's heavenly gifts…blissful with spirit and guidance,
Is a world blind by…*Vengeance and Ignorance*…now a witness
To the damnation of man…and in the sacrilege of his religions.

High on ramparts court…*do the fires of hell*…stay lit with torch,
As mankind continues his…*"Holy Wars"*…regardless life's cost.

And I fear…of mankind and his existence, all may soon be lost!

Blemishing the Bible's Truths….defying God's Commandments
Banishing its Gospels so written…and stoic to God's Covenants
Defiant of God's Sacraments…obeying instead…False Prophets
Inherent with *Original Sin*…and besieged into *evil's decadence.*

Am afraid the demise of mankinds existence has come to this!

In desecrating…"The Holy Scriptures"…from Station to Station,
His *ballots and bullets* have now bedamned mankinds salvation

While he places within our souls…*the wages of sin*…upon us all.
Shall heed he not to his call…so shall it be man's final downfall!

> Behold! The lies of the "Naysayer"…
> For they have been…God's betrayer
>
> Hold fast! Let man no longer bleed…
> And let now his path to heaven so be.

March forth no longer…onto the walkway's towards "Perdition"
Rather embrace one another with passion, love, and conviction
Then pray together in peace and hope for mankind's *contrition.*

Let all be blessed in grace…in serenity…and in "God and Glory".
And thus be fulfilled of God's decree…in freeing man's soul for

…All Eternity…

<u>…*After The Fall…Then The Rise*…</u>

When the final "Bastard Shells"…*reigns proud*…its fiery heat and shale
And *"The Stench Of Death's Disease"*…is breed…in the blood he breathed
Then *Man's Madness* will have prevailed…vilifying "Life's Balance Scale"!

Alas…Dear God! And *hear* my cries…For "After The Fall…Then The Rise"…

Smoked in ashes of debris…*burn the eyes and face*…of "Man's Atrocities"
In Molten Sands by the sea…*are the fallen erased*…by "Man's Machinery"
And across God's Land…*death stays busy*…in "The War Against Humanity"

Under wounding skies…*now lie yesterday's lives*…with fading memories…
Of flowering trees…with golden leaves! Of roses red…and gardens green.
And of *passion blue waters shimmering*…in the calm of an ocean breeze.

Uneasy now…do these waters rouse! *Corrupt*…and frothing so defiantly…
As *"Waves Interrupted"* are being *"Stormed and Thundered"* unforgivingly
And…*"Tides of Fire"*…erupt with ease! *Coloring Red*…this now violent sea!

By wars demand I stand in fear…on *Man's Barren Land*…naked and empty,
Wondering what more travesty…*still preys on the mind*…of Man's Insanity.

Alas…Dear God! And *heal* my cries…For "After The Fall…Then The Rise"…

Though "Wars Of Greed and Bigotry"…have "Castrated Man's Identity"…
And "The Hands Of Man's Technology"…has abbreviated time and history,
Man has failed by full decree…*in blaspheming*…"God's Manifest Destiny"!

So let he now rise against *evilry*…and yield not…unto the powers that be…
Nor…to their *"Clandestine Calvaries"*…ministering their sinister savagery.
Let he plunder man's cache of…*"Animus-Hostility"*… and all his weaponry.
And to the powers that were to be? To the sea…Ye bedamned! In Infamy!

As man flourishes again…so shall he rebuild and emend…Life's Civilization.
His lands will thrive…as *Nations Of Man*…strive for…"World Preservation."
He will promote *peace with salvation*…and pursue his "Moral Obligation"
To eradicate *bias and hate*… and man's acts of …"Genocidal Annihilation"!

As all wars end…shall "God and Man"…once again…"Rise After The Fall"…

…And "Balance Life's Scale"…For One And All…

Category Number Five

A Pendulum Of Evil...

...*In Tribute To E. A. Poe*

As there is much in the "Telling" lines of E.A.Poe's written works, it is in the "Untelling" words of the mind's eye, that so conjures up...his flames of Hell.

Shall then...may the following written iambic poems, shine-dark a "Tell"...into the abysm of thine own Hell!

J.J.R

Effigy To Poe

In wake of life's *"Untelling"* ages and of its *"Tellings"* in desperate times
Of life's revealing pages…*teared*…by the wind-swept splintering chimes
In written lines now faded…under stars silhouetted by the *Shaded Blind*
Lie fragments severed of Iron-Fisted Truths seen ladened heavy of mind.

And hauntings of a tortured soul stays burdened to its…heinous crimes!

Cursed with guilt! Am enflamed by the sordid pleasures in its bastardry
Consumed by drink! Intoxicated in its perfumes soiled within its revelry
Morbid memories unleashed…have unveiled a clouded feigned secrecy,
Of a conscience damned by repulsive scenes masking "True Identities"!

And the clays held Bust…to this Sculptured Beast…Ermined in Hypocrisy!

Embroided mirages once woven, now bleed this *"Telltale Heart"* its lies
With scissor-cut images crippled…"The Raven" crow beggars with cries,
In recoil of a young innocent tortured soul…nestled by life's false alibi's.

And the long-buried sins are now lain opened…in display of its disguise!

His silent echoes taunt still…this restless "Hyde"…
As mirrored demons are seen…aisled side by side
For deathknell's wrath as served…shan't be denied
Torment nevermor'…of this Lucifer brethren pride!

Naked now of these 'guises seen…is a mind diseased…mad with insanity
In wake of life's Mephisto dream…am chained "In-Hell" to thine enemy.

And empathy is now drawn in cries with pleas…poised in self-sympathy!

With corridors descending…with death being driven narrow of *"Trough"*
Crevasses unearthed have been *"Open-Graved"* by the *"Trident Plough"*.

Quietly, as I now drift in chamber…while "Satan" pounds his evil aloud…
Let thee put asunder thus evermor'…This Blood-Cloaked Devil's Shroud!

The Shattering Mirror

He who seeks solace within…His Hidden Stalls
Shall find of his plight…Memories Hidden Calls
For none can be cleansed of sin...In Hidden Lies...
As…"The Shattering Mirror"…Parades Hidden Lives!

J.J.R.

As I am cursed of the macabre…so I be damned in…*"Hell's Unholy Foray"*
While demons dine in *wanton delight* coveting yet another soul to prey.
Am I not to be ever set free of…*"The Evil Hand"*…choking me everyday…
Forever invading, forever depraving, forever be *"Deviling"* my life away?

Of Past *Sins Of Guilt*…In a world macabre…In a conscience now laid bare
Are stark visions of…*Spirits And Apparitions*…that follow me everywhere.
As no one hears my cries of pain…as no one sees *My Mirrors Of Despair*..
Accused I stay as…*The Eyes Of Persecution*…hold me witness to my fear.

So Temper I must…*"The Shattering Mirror"*…that *"Face"* my every stare!

With gift of breadth…With gift of Sight
With gift of strength…From Heaven's Light
Let Now God's Wrath…Shatter…"These Windows Of Fright"

…And Let Too…

His "Chariots of Angels"…Shatter Hell's…Macabre Mirrors of the Night!

Alas! No longer can I let…*These Mirrored Images*…paint me my destiny
And no longer shall I have…*These Scattered Pictures*…frame my misery
No longer too, shall…*My Blood Be Tainted*…by the Hell writhing in thee
No longer shall I see…*"The Mirror Shattering"*…for I have been set free.

Illusions seen within…*"The Looking Glass"*…through mirrored color eyes
Show deflections in *Prisms Macabre:* of a world in masquerade disguise.

So let now *"My Demons Sleep"*! Let macabre reflections be resolved
Let…*"My Emancipation Of The Soul Changeling"*…be finally absolved.

Shall not I be of fear! Let.."The Shattering Mirror"…vanish…disappear!

Shades Of Shadows

A Raging Inferno...has been burning away...at this flesh inside
Leaving scorched memories stranded frozen...etched in time;
While in body and soul..."The God's Of Hell"...revel with pride

And..."Shades Of Shadows"...play havoc...
...with "Demonic Delight"!

Of life's stolen moments...damned with Satan's indelible mark
Are eyes now teemed ashen...drawn in colors clouded of dark.

As the unhealed wounds are seen catalogued in naked display
A purloined mind is now clothed in sin...layered in evil's decay

And..."Shades Of Shadows"...
...Have now been served to darken...
..."The Sparrows Way!"

As another night of masquerading grandeur begins to subside...
Throes of despair; bathed in laughter could only modestly hide,
The lurid secrets kept of a heart...held captive...held chastised!

And on painted veil..."Shades Of Shadows"...
...Stay hauntingly alive!

With quieted pleas witnessed by plagued and saddened eyes...
This once *sainted soul* no longer can exist...pained or paralyzed
Nor poisoned by shame or guilt in angst to "The Devil's Lullaby".

And..."Shades Of Shadows"...have now bled dry
...Of the want...to survive!

So extinguish me these "Fires Of Hell"..."Its Disciples Of Devilry"
Take away too; this embattled life mired in hate and self misery

And let ..."Shades Of Shadows"...
...Forever be...
..."Helled Into Obscurity"!

The Unsainted Lost Soul

Born without spirit…is this soul unblessed
Poisoned by Satan's…"Dagger's Of Death".

Am Helled within the "labyrinth's of abuse"
While possessed by Evil's flagrant untruths.

In want of change…for the soul betrayed!

Rid me these Dagger's…on which I bleed
Uncloud my eyes…shine your light on me
Show me visions…of what life should be

Hand back my soul…and the spirits taken
Give unto thee… of The Christ forsakened

Allow me to embrace the love of another
Grant me Lord of an eternal life…together

Thus free me from these pains I now hold…
Being kept by…**"The Unsainted Lost Soul!"**

The Hell

As there is no one to give grieve...

...Let there be none see me bleed.

J.J.R.

Am felt of the cold wind breathing at my backside...at first unrealized
Am felt of the cold waters frozen...iced in pools of blood... in disguise
Am felt of the cold hand...being that of Satan's touch...at first denied
Am felt of the cold stares damning me...as I peer into its deviled eyes

Alive, yet am breached and void of body and spirit that once was free
Alive, yet am obliged by the plagues that are borne into this life to be
Alive, yet am entrapped in the forces of those evils...I'm meant to see
Alive, yet am felled to the *darkened nowhere* by the rise of my enemy

Echoes flaunt of waters shallow...lain hidden neath its blackened tide
Echoes haunt the soul once hallow...now aflamed by the sins of time
Echoes taunt...*This Face Of Pain*...being peeled naked from the inside
Echoes vaunt these...*Apparitions*...that hold hostage this *stolen mind.*

And I stay captive to these illusions...phantomed by my own design...!

Let sway this "Sword of Damocles" and cut with blade Satan's disease
Let thee vanish too; of this wraith...chanelled by...*"Hell's Menagerie"*...
Let me be lowered into sealed crypt...in waters free of "Hell's Enmity"

Let me thus be cleansed of sin...

...And of "The Hell"...

...That has come to swallow me!

Death's Trumpet

Let death be now so praised...
    ...To lighten thee thy weight...
        ...And thus release me my madness...
            ...Wreaked with its hate!

        J.J.R.

Within these cells of hate and sin...I've watched death's ghastly scenes.
In chairs electric...In chambers of gas...In death's...drugs of opportunity.
Obsessed now with death's disease...I stay held prisoner in my dreams.

As the "Voice of Hell" calls...as death screams beyond...darkened stalls
Bare I...my flesh. Bare I...my soul...Lay I...naked within my prison walls.

      And underneath the concrete green
      While slithering in its swamp debris
      Come... "The Harbinger's of Death"
      Lurking in the deep...in prey of me!

Suckled unto the breasts of Satan...am *Helled* into the depths of its evilry
So unburden thee this weight...let me now trespass unto Death's Destiny
And thus flay this hasty heart...this cursed soul...bleed me of this insanity.

For tonight...while under these muddied waters...as I face the sins of man
Shall I now taste of the guilt...in opened wounds...in carvings deft of hand.

Surrounded now, by The Face's of Death...
    ...Etched in driftwood's knotted knell...
        ...I stay ready to the sound of "Death's Trumpet"...
            ...As I descend unto the portals of its Hell!

Category Number Six

Odyssey: ...The Time And Travel*

            *The Spectrums Of...

Through all life's searchings...

        ...Through all his many journeys...

            ...Through all the lonely sojourns...

Never still...stands man's hopes...his dreams......nor his will...

"The Spectrum Of Time And Travel"...

        ...Has served as man's constant window...bearing witness...

            ...Unto...

"The Tellings And The Untellings"...kept alive and carried forward...

        ...Within each and everyone's very own...

"ODYSSEY"

The Human Sojourn

Prevailing through man's unsettling landscapes…while carrying life's light…
…In caravan{s} do they soldier forth…
…In quest…towards a better life.

Yes! The lost and displaced have *Sojourned* onward from countries torn…
…Saddled to meager belongings…broken dreams…
…And scarred by a world untoward.

Through-out the centuries…many have had to chart a changing course…
…As "The Fissures Of Fate"…had been fueled by war…
…While the teachings of man's ancient laws…
…Were being tainted and wronged!

And in "The Spectrums Of Time…And Travel"…
…"The Iliad"…of man's passage had been forewarned

His learned travels have witnessed…*the good, the faithful, and the bad*
Now; the eye's of life's knowledge has been set upon he; to take stand
For it is with purpose that "The Human Sojourn" unites freedom's flag!

And as…"The Human Sojourn"…shall traverse unto its "Final Odyssey"…
…So too; will man find his bonding truth…his common seed!

Lesson In Time

As our lives stay busy of so much to do
It seems the amount spent…"Quantity-Wise"
Never leaves enough time…for me…for you

However!

Times important "Essence"
May show a life worthwhile
If every man, woman, child

Indeed…

Would time a pregnant pause
To listen, to feel, to see
That life's values need not be
Measured only in "Time And Quantity"

…But Rather

In fulfilling life's blessings
Treasured in trove's of memories
In "Essence" to "Time And Quality"!

The Journey On

Every once in a great while a decency along with the whisper of humanity surfaces and the deluge of all that may show unbearable and insufferable becomes somehow tolerable, and with great applause, an appreciation of life is refreshed anew…

…For the journey must go on…

In a time of strong upheaval and lengthening moments seen perversed in conflicts, the thoughts for one to have concern for another has become a vanishing breed.

However, lo and behold…for when found and so discovered of another, a pocketful of hopes and dreams are shared and disillusioned am I no more. So I harken aloud in rejoice and prayer for man and decency still abounds. And once again has humanity been turned around.

…For the journey must go on…

And now, after all these years; I've been enriched anew…by the rare and endearing act of man's kindness being shown with genuine love and care. Within this seemingly unending odyssey of my walk through life, shall I so continue to ascribe evermore…of my steadfast concreted belief in regard to man's humanity and to the survival of his common decency…

…For The Journey Must Go On…

In Scenes of a Palatial Sphere Arising

Some exist maimed in cocoons silkened and wormed with intolerance
Some may exist tailored in clothes worn in mannered social ignorance
And some may exist in denial of effort circumventing ones emergence.

…For all however…

There exists compositional exponents given of spiritual convergence
Seen and held in host, possessive of an internal ethereal intelligence.

…Moreover…

The umbrella opening resurgent minds, can deliver a powerful creed
While breadth insurgent of "calibrated calculations" can be received
To coagulate growth in degrees of capabilities empowered to breed.

Let all be rid of the predilectory attitudes enslaved with intolerance
And let all divest the clothes worn and burdened in social ignorance
Then carry forth effort diligent in triumph…of ascending emergence.

…And thusly…

As an awakened "Goliath" shall go forth…
Then so too, shall a reawakened humanity become extinct no more.

And as mankind now grasps this new realm of a "Celestial Horizon"
All shall then prosper…

…*In Scenes of a Palatial Sphere Arising*

Category Number Seven

*Observations: ...A Diatribe...

...Of The Curiosities...*

Selection of essay's and shortened thesis and dissertations

on changing cultures...gender identities and its acceptance,

are but a few of the subjects broached in this next section.

Included are:

Identity: Part A & B

Part A

This day many can now give chance to their candid endeavours.
Venture anew in pursuit of life's surrounding natural pleasures.

With grandiosed bravado…and the purrs of freedom's essence,
There is need no longer of being held unto a captived audience
A new world is now crowned of colors painted in poetic justice.

Still, as issues of people's rights unfold…
                              …laws enacted take time to mold.

Many are seen to rush to judge, as they all stare so impatiently
While many turn their heads away, for they do not care to see:
The truth: of real love, its fidelity, nor of its "passionate purity".

            And many will *"stoop and sway"* with breeze…
            …In chasing their "implausable deniability"…
            …Protesting human rights…and life's liberties…!

As these walls are tearing down, voices are heard by all…finally
With new ground being broken, lingered doubts spread quietly.

Part B

Within hidden secrets there are equally hidden clues.
All need be cut opened…and be defined by its truths.

Alas my poor feline! For are you now ready to know?
Or will you still "cat". Though there is nowhere to go?

If…when you say: it's a new day, a new way, a new me,
Do be truthful to yourself and all, of your true identity.
As you will be asked of who, why, of what you may be!

For it is only of these choices, as you will come to see
That you can give your life…
                              …that will then "set you free"!

Provocative Thoughts

In this, the birth of our 21st Century, it has now been recognized that the precise definition of "manipulation" in its usages and associations can be cited as a malignant manifestation brought forward from its fore-runner spoken of in the past, which has been known to be that of the simplistic yet concise adage paraphrased:

"Oh, what a tangled web of lies we weave".

As man continues to apply underhanded tactics egregious of an ongoing deceit intended not for the fairness in right, but for their own egotistical satisfactions and personal advantages (at the expense of all), it thus has become abundantly clear that the adage: "It is man's inherent nature to hurt man", is a reality of horrific proportions, severe consequences, and extenuating circumstances.

Subsequently, a fine "art" has, in this new technological age, been filled with "Voice-Boxes"…espousing their own interpreted viewpoints. Their "opinions", its "explanations", and the "answers", (here-to-forth), have no relativity to the questions asked nor of the subjects involved.

And as such, this fine "art" has now developed into a "tool of deception". We have been blinded to the "Sell" attached to these central themes. A well-roundedness inclusive of: transparency and plain language, has now given all, subliminal messages via "Untelling"…notice's of "manipulation with intent to deceit"!

All have now taken place…"in new face"…of another euphemism of olde

"One lie begets another lie, which begets yet another lie" and so on. We recognize such quote as to its truest meaning and of its deepest cut.

Of An Opinion

Of the many sensitive issues that are and have been debated in heated discussions, I mention this particular one that has me somewhat aghast.

It seems the idea of a "marriage" by two people having the same sexual preferences and are biologically the same sex, does not sit well with the so-called good standings within the covenants of church and state as so enacted in and of the laws and rules so deemed by man and God.

Serious considerations need be brought forward in an open forum for a public hearing as to the concerns of the people's outcry for: Gay Rights. Reasons abound as to the issues and its importance in todays society.

As this is a different age in time, attitudes and ethics in moral standings have evolved. Such perspectives need to be voiced in that regard. Man-made laws of yore must be amended to level the rights for all people to have fair and equal opportunities in all endeavors for survival.

As a simple man, I can only suggest that a case for *"joined partnerships"* being formed for/and within…a matrimonial unionization between two people of the same sex…that are in love with one another and carry the same values and are willing to be bonded by the same vows as married couples, should thus be allowed to do so.

Such purpose, reason, and proposal, for an enacted amendment to the "Constitution" should be recognized with written definitions espousing economic, and social freedom so drawn to all people. Common-sense-dictates it should be mandatory for these proposals to be….so ordered. (on record).

* Since "Of An Opinion" written May 5, 1999, a host of laws and court rulings have been enacted throughout the "States of America".

** Processes for acceptance has also reached across the seas to other nations.

Category Number Eight

*Ah! All Seriousness Aside: In Serendipity...

...A Bit Of Brevity-Levity-And Joy*

These next three subjects are shortened

versions of writings that may put a smile

on the face of the young and the curious.

Included are:

Formula For A Winning Team

In assembling a group of talented individuals into a cohesive "Unit Of One" and then melding all to grow and mature together through the processes' of teachings and through the experiences of failures and successes are the initial ingredients that applies to the "Formula For A Winning Team".

When all players listen to learn and coaching staffs apply their expertise in "observe and teach", and they too, listen to learn, then another ingredient for the "Formula For A Winning Team", thus starts to churn.

A building block for winning, is for a team to "Jell". There is a "Chemistry" that is at first unseen nor "Force-Fed". It begins magically with all; slowly developing while eventually carrying forward with its "Leaps and Bounds". The players, the coaches, and the manager too, become that "Chemistry" that "Jells" to play as a "Team Of One"…and now that season has begun.

During the course of a teams seasonal play, mental maturity and a mutual admiration for all begins developing and takes hold. With each day's trial and tribulation that abounds for every team with everyone, a progression towards fruition indeed takes its role. As such, a team has now been mold, and a respect is seen collectively by all. Thus all are reminded of the focus of their goal. Justly, the effort of working as a unit now becomes that key ingredient so essential in the "Formula For A Winning Team".

Part of the "Formula For A Winning Team" still, are the skills and talent of the management and personnel. "Behind The Scene" and "Off The Field" decisions and its "Handling And Timing" are important factors as all are in search for the ultimate dream.

In order to implement management's program and for all to "buy into the premise"; all are needed to be…"On The Same Page". Therefore, another ingredient needed for the "Formula For A Winning Team", is the ability to know when and how to "Process And Execute". All are ingredients under the "Umbrella" held of "Patience, Attitude, Poise, and Composure".

A lasting ingredient needed for the "Formula For A Winning Team"…to be so acclaimed…is what is aptly termed as having…"For Love Of The Game"!

Sayings One Way Or Another

"The Only Thing That Never Changes...
...Is Change Itself"...

However, "The Only Thing That Does Change...Is Change"...

While Another Saying Is: "Six Of One...
...A Half-Dozen Of Another"...

Above gives credence to the full meaning of this saying...

"The More Things Change
...The More They Stay The Same"...

Coincidentally, "Some Things That May Be Seen...
...Are Not Necessarily What They Appear To Be"...

Perhaps this could be a direct reflection of the saying...

..."You Can't Judge A Book By Its Cover"...

So remember "To Not Lay Judge Of A Man...
...Until You've Walked A Mile In His Shoes"...

In life as one gets along in years and loses track of time, one tends to take these clichés, sayings, and truisms, for granted. However, the young, the ones who may be "Knee-High To A Grasshopper", may not yet be aware of these sayings or perhaps their full measure in its messages and meanings.

For all; I give of this "Golden Nugget" of which I live by:
For..."As One Learns...So then...Shall One Teach"...

The Oxymoron-Paradox Adaptation

In the "Dark Of The Day" one may find "A Light At The End Of The Tunnel"
Though one may say…"Some Things Seen Are Not As They Appear To Be"
Keep in mind: "The More Things Change…The More They Stay The Same".

Above written examples are expressions specializing in the titles given to
Phrases and sayings, adages in proverbs, and in spoken words of truisms'.
Verses written below will exhibit…"The Oxymoron-Paradox" euphuisms…
As told in storylines; fact or fiction, and with mock congruent aphorisms!

In the evolutionary realm of time, the human intellect has equally grown.
Favoring all with tools of knowledge and in wisdom never before known.
Man, with his ever-expanding intuitive mind, envisions himself in control.

So too, according to our scholars of science and our theoreticists of old…
Is our universe still-expanding, still-advancing, …still-growing, on its own.

All may lend credence to the tune…."It's A Big Wide World…We Live In"!

With all our Laws of physics and its properties…still not yet fully scrolled
With all of Mother Nature's Earth…unleashing its wrath across the globe
With all of man's continued distrust of each other throughout the world
Let truth be told! Man has not truly grown, nor ever had he true control

We are drowning dry…"Our Open Waters" and natures…"Ebb and Flow".
We contrive to master all in…"Closed-Minds"…yet our "Eyes" still show,
Our hidden vagaries and volitions to have been so…unwittingly exposed.

With…"Big Brother Watching"…and each other's business revealed to all
"It's A Big Wide World"…now appears to be a world growing quite small!

So has been fashioned by these observations, provocative in application
Prosed with verse ascribing to: "The Oxymoron-Paradox"…Identification.

Therefore, a proven theorem in print should now exist with verification…

…Of…"The Oxymoron-Paradox-Adaptation"…

Category Number Nine

Of Life's Journey...So Cometh Man's Learnings

Included in this selective category are the following:

As the ...table's of time...have been thrust upon man...

So too...shall his capacity and want for knowledge...

...Continue to expand...

Life's Essential Keys

Within the *slice's* of one's journey through life…there exists challenges, decisions, and changes. How we view them and how we react towards each given episode of *confrontation and conflict* as its circumstances are so presented, will invariably set in motion "Life's Essential Keys". These "Essential Keys" of life will be pertinent *building blocks* in determining one's…*character.* And as such, developmental growth with maturity will give provision to several necessary components. Maintaining *composure* and *restraint* with *balance and strength,* will lend further to one's *sense of definition.* These are but a few of…"Life's Essential Keys"…one shall need to be in possession of…for they will collectively elicit *stature* to one's "Self-Being".

All questions that are needed to be asked and answered…need be done; with *thought of scope,* and with serious consideration to its *depth* and within its *breadth.* Recognition of consequences in one's decision and ensuing *ramifications and repercussions* are one of "Life's Essential Keys".

Another of…"Life's Essential Keys"… one may need to nurture, is known as…*self-confidence.* It will give…*shoulder to self-esteem*…and eventually evolve into…*the will, want, and the desire,* in bettering oneself. Seek then of this "Key" and thus apply an earnest effort to develop, and…to cultivate, and then employ the thirst needed for knowledge and the taste for its understanding.

As one experiences the *passage's of life*… there is a need for one to not only *breathe of the air,* but to *breathe in the awareness of*… all that encompasses their surroundings. This "Key"…may allow for one to give pause and thus to hold of the joy and to wisely take in the *beauty and the passions* given of love and adventure. Enjoy too, life's provocative casual interludes and thusly be enthused and stay enthralled to life's creative juices. Be curious and intrigued unto all life's mysteries and wonders…as your journey continues throughout the passing years.

Existing yet is another "Key"…when one is faced with life's obstacles and of one's adversaries. Previously mentioned as the "Key" called *composure and restraint*; as it induce's patience and enforces focus. However, this "Essential Key"…is akin to maintaining control and in exercising compromise…when one is or may be confronted with life's sudden conflicts. And it is akin to; when displayed in proper and obliging form: "The Key" that gives call to *Respect and Attitude.* It extends *breadth in balance,* and enlightens one's perception as in…"*Steering an Even Keel*".

Know it is not quite enough to only give *voice*…in aim for one's goals. There is and will be the need to have the ability to empower within oneself, "Life's Essential Key" that enables one to envelop *sustained perseverance.* Ethics in work, and in its quality will enfuel protocol in one's procedure. This "Key" is needed to be endured as one follows forth accomplishing said goals.

As life will *paint picture's* of its *ebb's and flow's*…grab hold onto these…"Essential Keys". For they give measure in meaning and in lesson's worthy to their value. And they will give "*lead*" as one prepares oneself for "The Long Run Down The Winding Road" that is known as "LIFE"!

Pondering of Thoughts
...Part One...

1) Let one need be both aware nor dismissive of "The Doubter's" and "The Naysayer's". There is explanation for cause and reason...right or wrong. Be cognizant of the positive's and negative's you face, for words empty, will never show lasting promise or grace.

2) One should take heed to the words so spoken with Conviction In Belief, and to those that take responsibility; not only for their actions, but also for their assertions. Recognize too, the one's that remain accountable, for when proven wrong; they will offer forth dignity and humility...with a true and genuine apology for all that may have been stated and acted upon previously.

3) Not all is necessarily aplenty for the many that may take delight as they traverse along on "The Primrose Path". But, of the earnest few that do believe in paving their own way...the cobble road that forks to the right, will lead them onto..."The Path's Of Opportunity". There is not a better feeling, than to appreciate not only the satisfaction of working, but...of learning, and in earning one's way in life, and as well; in how far and to what goals can one achieve. *The ladder of success* stands in your reach.

4) Similar in theme and conviction...I have stayed with want coupled to the ideals and beliefs that has been endured...as has been stated previously. As I'm often witnessed by "The Faces Of Folly"; I have shadowed my way through "The Eye's Of Life's Journey"...standing steadfast and pondering of what roads to travel. Inspired, I take notice to the wondrous rewards to be gained as one combines tenacious effort and determination. Then applies dedication in due-diligence, and in duty, drive, and diversity. All with a fiery desire in fulfilling those life time wishes. Let then these host of assets be thus "Filed And Catalogued" into one's "Library Of Dreams"!

5) At great expense of self, have I now come to know: *For every garden to grow...a little rain must soon fall.* And so shall cometh of these throes', are trials and tribulations, and the love's touched and let go, and of the sorrow and the pain so felt through it all that doth bring us whole unto the watchful eye of "The Endeavour's Call". Its "Tapestry Of Emotions" with its make-up and designs that all shall experience across a timeline of "Life's Great Divide"...shall provide shape and structure to character, and thus emanate an essence needed in creating one's own self-being!

Continue...

6) The ways of life are complex and the created imaginings of the mind hinges on the intriguing paradigm's that are bound to develop along one's journey. So take notice into…"The Tellings And The Untellings" that appear seemingly quite profound by their meanings and in their abstract expressions that are seen "glympsed" by the following lines:

     (1) "Oh!...But For The Path Not Taken"…
     (2) "As You Come To The Fork In The Road"…
     (3) "I'll Cross That Bridge…When I Come To It"!
     (4) "No One Likes Being Put In Harms Way"!
     (5) "Stuck Between A Rock And A Hard Place"!

7) Perspectives and proper utilization will give aid that may dictate and enhance worded reasonings to serve purpose for the need and want in one's daily decision-making. "Process, Execution, and Elimination" shall thus become the "Pillar Of Strength"…in guiding your directives.

8) "Cause and Effect": A term that has much significance. For when one becomes deft in understanding its powerful message, and recognizes its consequences and its results lay in their hands, they subsequently find themselves geared to be…"One step ahead of the game". To all who may not be familiar with this term, and of its hidden definitions and multi-faceted meanings, take time to study. It will pay off.

9) One need exude a quiet…yet dignified presence while abiding to the social manner's shown of grace and reverence in protocol to respect. One should also take heed in drawing attention upon oneself. Take pause and then listen, think, and learn, as words are said often with hidden meanings…and in "Double Entendre's" given to …hyperbole!

10) Take it upon yourself to give pause in thought to the expression that states: it may be beneficial and more than admirable in taking a step back, and a deep breath, saying to yourself, I'm glad I'm not like him. Know too…at times, patience and understanding can wear thin. Now let us all take a step back, and let the following become man's creed:

"Never judge a person unless you have walked a mile in their shoes".

Guidelines: Stepping Stones

(1)   Never allow yourself to be put in a position...
              ...that you may not be able to extricate yourself from.

(2)   Never a crisis...always a solution...(P.M.A.) = Positive Mental Approach.

(3)   Take time to concern yourself with others...
              ...Perspectives in perceptions will flourish then fulfill.

(4)   Never underestimate your opponent...nor ever over-estimate yourself.

(5)   As one becomes greedy...one becomes careless...then one gets caught.

(6)   Sometimes as one becomes too smart...they can outsmart themselves.

(7)   Being unduly impressionable and unduly gullible...is unduly acceptable.

(8)   Always weigh your options...then be comfortable with your decision(s).

(9)   Do not jump to conclusions...do not presume to assume...nor guess.

(10) Be cognizant of alleged evidence's...and of the *absence of evidence(s)*.

(11) Be true unto thy self...for through-out life...truth will always win-out.

(12) No short-cuts to success...*overnight success* takes many years of work.

(13) When at a seemingly disadvantage...find the advantage. Therefore seek.

(14) Intrigue yourself with life...its surroundings...its curiosities, its mysteries.

(15) Take it upon yourself: to listen, to learn, to experiment, to experience.

(16) Discipline your mind...focus your thoughts...let *common-sense* prevail.

The Employee Criterion

As all new employees embark into their workplace environment…there will be workforce rules, standards, and required ethics that are needed.

Thus take note of the following:

Each individual employee should possess qualities that not only show performance of job tasks, but also includes levels of knowledge in the understandings of such requirements and of the reasons for its needs, merits, and outcome.   **"ACCOUNTABILITY"**

Overview and general intuitiveness are qualities that each individual employee will need and to perfect. Application of skills will be in use for certain varied job duties that may have underlying hidden factors which may not be visible nor viable at said time of execution. Albeit: reading between the lines.   **"PERCEPTIVENESS"**

A skill each individual employee should come to develop further with experience, is to recognize "ramifications and repercussions" of their actions taken or lack thereof. Prepare yourself to always think ahead.
                              "BEING AWARE"

In the workplace environment an individual employee may be asked to handle multiple job tasks in a given day. All are aware of multi-tasking. A wide range of one's abilities will be roundly and routinely utilized. A high level of skilled "work habits and ethics" are required for every job. Quick-study and focus of attention will be needed in covering all tasks at hand. I.E. info-data processing…tele-communications, and "On-call" work platforms for incoming and/or outgoing work-orders.
                              "DIVERSIFICATION"

It is imperative for each individual employee to have qualities that are indicative…of self-assuredness and self-esteem. There may be certain duties and operations that one may not fully understand. Sometimes, direction from another is needed to carry forward a job or task…to its completion. In being an (invaluable) employee, do not hesitate to ask assistance. It is not viewed in any manner as incompetency. Instead… it elicits an admirable trait given of inner strength. **"SELF-CONFIDENCE"**

All individual employees pay special attention of this reading. In time all may become the recipients of.."**Lessons Taught, Lessons Learned!**"

Keys To Business – The Workforce Toolbook

Many will eventually enter the world of business. Some may aspire to be in business for themselves while others may be satisfied working for someone else. "Key" factors will be involved whether one becomes the employee or the employer, for a successful career to be achieved along the way.

The following are guidelines for the "Keys To Business" that may be used as a "Workforce Toolbook". Employee, laborer, sales, management, employer; whatever the job title…know there will be various "Keys" necessary to each classification that may successfully guide you in the right direction.

Completing a well-rounded education is part of one's package. As nothing exceeds the studying, the book readings, nor its learned lessons taught by teachers, professors, and scholars, during one's years of schooling.

However, as you enter the workforce environment, you enter yet another phase of learning tangent to your schooling. It advances further the "Key" needed for success. It is termed: "On The Job Experience". It will provide a plethora of knowledge in your now new working-class environment, and will give a full understanding of the requirements essential for business.

The following lists consists of ten…

…"Keys To Business – The Workforce Toolbook"…

(1) Whether employer or employee, always be cognizant of the manner as to how you wish to represent yourself. Discipline, confidence, and controlled composure can exude stability…and an awareness as you begin to interact with others in the workplace. Your interactions will therefore be accepted as you project perception with capability. Subsequently, all others will take notice in your behavior and with how you're able to "self-maintain", all the while…commanding a respect with a presence of strength. As time passes, you will come to understand the term: "A Delicate Balance".

(2) Learn to know how and when to apply "Limitations" in your dealings as an employer or an employee. Over-extending oneself or that of the business, is a casualty that can prove quite detrimental for success to be realized.

Continue…

(3)   Situations from time to time arise where "Levity" is needed as a panacea for easing tensions amongst co-workers, and/or management. Working hard, working late, or side by side in an enclosed area, can give cause for tempers to flare-up. As the proprietor or the manager in charge, you are responsible for handling and halting any outbursts or uprising. As such, a "Key" for success…is knowing your personnel and changing environment, and when to respond with a timely respite of "Levity" to "Stem The Tide". Sometimes it is necessary for all to share in a…"Little Give And Take"!

(3)   Tangent with #3 above, whether you are the employer or the employee, (as in management or sales), know your customer. A "Key" ingredient in success will include your abilities to assess the needs and wants, and the likes and dislikes, of your consumers, associates, and clientele. Be aware of variable personalities and then appease accordingly. For in that vein… an increase in sales, productivity, and repeat business, will spell success.

(4)   For the business-owner known as the "Proprietor", several "Key" facts are essential for maintaining a successful operation. First and foremost, know your business inside-out…and in the direction you wish for it to move into. Secondly, understanding supply, demand, profit margins, and the ensuing bottom-line, will be a focal point you must grasp…as you quest forward in building a viable and stabled business. Thirdly, as the business-owner, be aware of obligations and the risks in decision-making. Being accountable, responsible, and having a vision of purpose, are exemplary traits for one's continued effort to procuring a successful and prosperous business.

(5)   As a business-owner-operator, it is also of utmost importance to be able to recognize "Deadweight". Equally important is to act quickly and to rid yourself and your business if it…quietly! Common Sense and Instinct can play as key factors for both an employer and the employee as well. They include: create calm and not chaos, simplify not magnify, do not hurry to conclusions, and these two adage's: "It don't need fixin' if it ain't broke", and that one should be…"Part of the solution, not part of the problem"!

Your gut, timing, and a bit of luck, can be "Keys" for all in the workplace.

Continue…

Keys To Business – The Workforce Toolbook

(6)   Addressing work production, assessing efficiency, and assigning qualified personnel to be able to handle their shifts without incident, are the basic requirements necessary for management to possess. However, it is one's employer who has the ultimate responsibility in having their business run smoothly and as efficient as possible. Therefore, the hiring of employee's with "The Right Stuff" is a strong and important "Key" in business success.

(7)   In hope of achieving success in the business world, be it as the employer or the other fields mentioned as titled in and of the workforce personnel, it will be beneficial to understand this next particular…"Key": All need to be aware that it is a "Team" that brings about success in business. It is a "Unit Of Cohesive Players" with an intertwining matrix held by employer-employee ideals, idea's, and advise's and consents being meted-out as in "Round-Table" discussions that can and will spew forth business growth, along with one's own personal growth as well. When understood by all, it is achieved without…"Ego" and/or "Deception", but rather with honest effort and with dignified integrity. It should be a concept-principle, that all should employ.

(8)   A "Key" or rather a "Golden Nugget", whether an employee or employer, is to keep in mind that Perception Begets Comprehension and vice-versa. So give pause for thought in contemplation…as you successfully attempt to move ahead in the workplace-world of business.

(9)   Utilize the "Tools" you have thus far learned, and hone them to the best of your abilities, then apply them to the job tasks as needed. Remember there are more "Tools" to hone as you further along. So learn!

Much information indeed may prove invaluable through the years. Not only in use for "Keys To Business-The Workforce Toolbook" but as well…

…"For The Keys Of Life"…

Category Number Ten

In Random: Networking The Matrix Perspective

Oh! Of the complexities…perplexing mankind

The subject material written for this section

Intimates hints of a controlled manipulation

In the evolving changes man has brought to…

…Not Only…

Today's Machiavellian-Like Machinations

…But To…

The Innocence of…"Yesterday's Children"!

Of Case In Point: Part One

As comprehension begets perception, and (vice-versa), one finds there may exist many that dwell in continuous reiterations versed in redundant rhetoric. Information and instructions with concerns to conversations and discussions in agreements and/or rebuttals need be concise and accurate. When there is the need for classified and intrinsic personal data to be delivered and negotiated, it must be done in an orderly fashion and performed by qualitative reliable individuals.

Of grave importance to each, when disseminating, assigning, or delegating oral or written allocutions from one or more sources to another or others, it need be so guaranteed to be correctly handled and specifically managed to its conclusion. These tasks are to be exacted by highly qualified and by highly respected professionals in their chosen fields of expertise. All should have in their possessions, those attributes consistent with the previously mentioned: comprehension in perception, etc. There will be aspects further to discuss concerning this subject, that will be delved into as we continue along.

The meanings of said written statements above may be defined apropos to the understanding of the following statements written below, congruous to subject matter titled: "Of Case In Point: Part One".

The individuals that have such acumen mentioned above, have also developed the learned ability to listen and the capacity to do so astutely with steadfast focus and paralactic intensity. Subsequently, subtracted from their lives are insipid portions of the unnecessary and inconsequential uselessness.. of time consumption, wasted energy, and the needless complications given to repetitious innuendo.

Today we find there exists still, unconscionable acts, ambivalent to attitude and function, anointing a condescendence to flagrant incompetency and sustainable ineptness…being foistered further with unpretentious behavior, dismissing effort, and lack of concern for their acts. Thus giving satisfaction to compromise, misconduct, and mismanagement of: business, government, and society, in general.

All have given rise infused with prowess unpararalleled in complacent comfortability. Inured by this phenomena is the machinations now seen to excuse personal formalities and submit instead, a crude and impersonal indignity and arrogance now sliced in quadrants beheld not of accountability and/or responsibility…, but rather in steadfast plausible deniability. Thus leaning towards the trickled down and over-exposed meaningless "slogans" falsely broadcasted to the masses of "checks and balances", "plain language", and "transparency". All under the umbrella guised by "political diplomacy" and/or "political correctness". Take into accord that these "Hidden Lies" will be recognized and recorded in our annals…for "Truth in Reality" does not stay buried.

Time has come today for a semblance of order; a conviction of truth in the beliefs of justice; morality given of tradition with genuine honesty; and an invested effort for a people to regard accountability, and societal responsibility as the characteristics so represented in earlier times that had forwarded a nation to enjoin internal strength, stability, and a patriotic duty…in its ethics…as so conceived and so envisioned, by our…" Founding Forefathers".

"Of Case In Point": such is the need for comprehension / perception and for all to gain understanding with a continued effort in educating oneself.

Continue…

Of Case In Point: Part Two

It is now apparent that all have been subtly force-fed (sub-consciously) via-manipulative subliminal messages, into embracing this current 21st century world of high-finance, greed, and self-indulgence. The evidence's brought forth into the open, through the various modems of media-news exposure have given notice that many of the leaders of the day had been doing so in steps "covered up", consistent with malicious acts and questionable intent.

Even now, as we enter the mid-point first quarter century mark of this new millennial...our leaders, ministers, and other world councils of advisors, are still seen conspiring via underhanded ploys in their attempts to continue to badger (devious acts) in manners and behaviors indicatively based on false pretenses.

A Case In Point: Part Two-A

With a constant agenda veiled in corruption of ethics at the very core, we can paint a poisonous face shown to be disarmingly antithetical; contrary to the frame-work proposed and set forth by our "Forefathers" as stated: "A Government For The People, By The People, And Of The People"...ETC.

Those written truths dignified by the signatures of our "Founding Fathers" on their documents, have held steadfast as our "Canons"...now known as: "The Declaration Of Independence"..And.."The Constitution Of The United States Of America". All have bonded a nation, a culture, a civilized society, for some 240+ years. We need not "sway" nor "stray" from these "truths".

Laws of Man and God have been emended within our initial Constitutional frame-work, as time, attitudes, cultural diversity, and our civilized societal-principles have advanced forward. Thus improving on change consistent to humanitarian conditions focused on uniformity and equality in, and of, and for, the rights of people all. "The Articles Of Freedom" may come to mind.

Separation of Church, State, and Religious Rights of Freedom, have and are still being amended with "bi-laws" being redefined, proposed, and revised, through the frame-work of our "Constitution Of The United States", and to our "Declaration of Independence".

As such: "ALL MEN AND ALL WOMEN...ARE CREATED EQUAL".

Continue...

Of Case in Point: Part Three

Reasons for these previously written diabtribe's come to light as many will undoubtedly gain an insight into the total spectrum of what we have so far been witnessed to (in this scenario) as so "designed" to have brought forth all people's into today's troublesome quagmire's of unrest, conflicts, chaos, and disorder (now worldwide).

…Read on…for there is more to grasp…

Leaders of many nations are now interwoven with each other via treaties, pacts, and so-called alliances. They have "founded" anew, the notion that a "New World Order", would enhance further, of their own governmental control and power within their "Ministries Of Justice". They will continue the past evils of "Money", "Ego", "Power", and "Greed", as a history shall once again repeat itself. They have, and are still seen walking in the same "footsteps" first analyzed with observation, and then finally implemented with manipulative tactical maneuvers used for deception…employed by a changing world. The resulting procedures stitched by the "ties that bind", would soon paint false perceptions eying an…"Advanced Shared Society". However, lost "in transition", were the ethics to service equalized growth for this "Globalizing Governmental Solidarity". As time has pressed forth, reality has finally spoken:

"SOMETHING WAS AMISS"!

Transgressions and inadequacies with skewed notions in ideals both true and false…that leaders have bended with transparency in its rhetoric and hyperbole have surfaced to serve sad notice. Its cause and effect of such incendiary actions, empty words, and disingenuous promises, that so led many to be lulled into a "Deep Sleep", is now being finally reawakened.

"Of Case In Point", as a history will provide an ear to the public. It's truth shall indeed uncover that we, the people of America, hath let flow far too long, the constant and continuous unspeakable and manipulative acts: of *"our leaders"…and…"our government".*

No more is there time to sleep nor to stay "Oblivious In Comatose State". It is for us to "Pound The Hammer" and to revive anew…the many truths indoctrinated within our nation, by and of, our "American Constitution", so framed and written for all, as set forth by our "Forefathers".

Continue…

Of Case In Point: The "Addendum"

Acts forwarding secret negotiated brokered deals engaged by all parties, had not the weight, nor worth, of the paper that it was written on. With many "hands in the pie", too many extended tentacles gave opportunity for a continuum of corruption in ethics that spoke of the so-called, "new-norm" that stayed in play with its basic adage indicative of man's lust for:

"MONEY, POWER, AND GREED".

Thusly, all parties began exhibiting a more powerful secreted motivation. Unfortunately, these actions were never maneuvered to function for the "Good Of The Whole".

With that being said, all should now be apprised of this all out consuming pandemic unrest as caused by "Money, Power, And Greed" that has been metastasizing into "revolts of revolutionary" status throughout the world. All should realize this domino effect and its delusional visions of grandeur and ego; for it has been seen in man's existence throughout time. Simply said, once again, of a **"HISTORY REPEATING ITSELF"**!

Be it known as well, is to grasp the understandings of this phraseology as spoken by an acknowledged and well acclaimed doctor of medicine (and) analytical forensics: **"SOMETHING WRONG WITH THIS PICTURE"**!

All will give meaning to the realization of this adage so profoundly noted: "Lying In Bed With Your Enemies"! Know too, they're "Lying In Bed" with you! Sooner or later, for all involved, no good shall be "gotten" for it has been said...

"IT IS MAN'S INHERENT NATURE TO DESTROY MAN!"

Chess Games

An adversarial coalition has quietly mounted its game plan to perfection. As they have fortified their strengths with additional *Players* that have so placed the United States Of America on the same *Enemy List.*

These adversaries have built and are methodically building with voracious ferocity, an unprecedented...*arsenal of hatred*...against our western world culture. And with intensified resolved determination...and an accelerated pace, this now organized army has taken to widespread actions consisting of total devastation and attempts at complete: *Genocidal Annihilation.* Be assured, that continuous further acts of disruption will ensue...not only on the lands of our allies, but on our very own homeland as well. Be it known there has been an on-going Chess Game being played and is now entering what has been termed as "The Middle Game". Know too, there is much in this equation that will indeed be fleshed out as time presses onward.

A brotherhood of factions, which includes the newly named trifecta, known as *"Alquerda-The Taliban-*and *Issil,"* are and have been growing steadily and expanding rapidly. Attention has been acrimoniously heightened via (24/7) broadcastings being aired publicly through-out the world. Consequently, a steady flow of disheartened, disillusioned dissidents, including undesirables from all countries and tribal nations have been and are continuing to join in on what will eventually become the..."Jihadists Military Terrorist Army"!

For those blind and for those that refuse to witness of the aggressions and carnage taking place by these evil acts of mankind, and thus so chooses to *Turn the other cheek*...be aware! For not only have we *stayed too long...at the dance,* we have verily *played too long a losing gambit*, vying for control within a "Middle Game" positioning of this true life and death Chess Game.

As for the last two decades? All are and have been confronted by this now impending reality of an East-West religious and cultural war that may have the impetus to evolve into the "Proselytized Armageddon" as written in its Holy Bibles. The threats and the actuality of a W.W.III are real!

The next moves to be made in this...Game Of Chess, may very well dictate, what is known as "The End Game"!

Note: 1st released in 2012*

And as time forages onward, it is not only "Innocence" that has become "Extinct". It is I as well…   J.J.R.

"The Last Dinosaur"

Moments of reflection have led me to realize the loss of traditions and spirit in the values once held, that emboldened strength and tenacity… unifying a fledgling young nation of long ago, to eventually become an America of today.

Of recent times…cries for morality, civility, integrity, and workman-like ethics have been progressively cast asunder. In its place are aggressive "voices", active in its oratory, equivocating to an indulgent impersonal:

"Machine Oriented Automated World".

This age of "Trans-Technology" is seen being faceted within the global communication borne through a computerized networking matrix. Its signature is seen giving advanced tellings of an "A.I." world fomenting at an accelerated and unprecedented pace.

As such, the "everyman" has now become lost in transition, and so too, "lost in translation". A Loss of principles and respect has bled us into a world seemingly insensitive of compassion in its peoples and attitudes. Suggestions of complacency designed in theory as a model of efficiency in warranting the widespread use of "the machines of intelligence", are effectively causing the extinction of the everyday "layman".

We've now lost an appreciation in the innocence of naivete, youth, and the traditional family values that once brought all together. Many have failed to recognize each other, and many have moved too fast…without experiencing those "stepping stones" engaged in our youthful journeys.

Of "The Last Dinosaur"…I seem bound to be, I stay saddened in all I see. For across this new world enslaved in "Machinery"… are forgotten joys of youthful times once held by all…so innocently!

Continue…

Innocence Extinct
"The Last Dinosaur"

In youthful times as I recall…children young and old would share their gifts with one and all. A bicycle, a doll-house, or perhaps a book of stories, or a book to color your stories in. These tales they told would bring smiles and laughter "innocent" to every boy and girl. Sugar plums and candied apples *would dance in their eyes and onto the pages read…while young wandering* minds would begin to think ahead "To What Dreams May Come"…and then to explore…*"In Visions Of Grandeur"*…!

As small wonders began to fascinate…and to excite a young child-like mind, thoughts began to form while ideas began to "shine". Thus summoning up a "taste for appetite"…and a desire that yearned to learn more. Ah! Those were the times I remember of yore…before I became "The Last Dinosaur"!

Oh! Whatever did they do to that world of Innocence which I once knew?

I remember, too, as I continue to forward through in this forever-changing passage of mine; when it was a "radio" that was the "voice" and the center of attention, albeit…the main attraction for everyone to "hear" at the time.

Family member's of the "household" would all gather and then sit around to listen, enjoy, discuss, or perhaps opine in glee, or in friendly quarrel and then in harmony; of these "radio-talk" personalities pitching their repartee. Yes! "All in the Family"…would tune in each day, just to listen to its variety of shows and the programs that "The Radio" would put on display.

There may be programs of mystery or melodrama's with perhaps a tinge of music playing in the background, effecting a subtle suggestion heightening suspense, or an onset event; sudden in surprise. And as we all listened, our imaginations would arise.

It could be a program with an on-going theme. A western serial, or a scary thriller enticing sighs, cries, and/or screams. It may be a call-in radio show or perhaps a comedy to muse or be amused by. All would give fancy to the minds young and old, of dreams and visions, and imaginings in thoughts yet to unfold.

Continue…

Innocence Extinct
"The Last Dinosaur"

I can remember too, during those "golden radio days", how movie-houses began to play host in much the same way. "Story-telling"…was now being visually shown in picturesque beauty for all to behold. Actor and Actress, and those behind the scenes honed their skills in this "acting craft", being known and seen as…

"Movie Magic-Making Artistry"!

Yes, this new medium projected on the big screen, the magnificence of the world outside our own; to be seen within…the imaginations of our dreams. And today I ponder: Am I "The Last Dinosaur" now too old…to blind to see? For I am afraid there have been far too less of these "Story-telling" moving pictures being told to me; in today's power-driven "money-hungry" movie-making…Industry.

There was a time I remember of long ago, when another "new medium"… called "Television"…would become known to one and all. Neighbors and friends came together to sit down on the "parlor floor"…and watch "T.V.". Shown on this home screen were comedy routines, music, song and dance acts…westerns, news, and everything in between.

Yes! On a "parlor room floor"…entertainment was enjoyed by one and all.

Memories spring to mind of thoughts when in earlier times, a world would recognize of the genius bestowed in the stylings and the imageries imbued. The artists, the painters, the sculptors and impressionists too…whom, with hands of clay and brushes of colour would so stroke onto canvasses and so caress on pedestals, their artistic vision for all to see. All would endeavour in paint and sculpt of imaginings…ever so breadth-taking with its creativity.

Remember too, in days of old…when baseball and football were games of fun and played that way for everyone? Time and greed has since coursed on as money has now become the goal, so ending the games, and the loss of fun once enjoyed by all.

…And today I cry aloud. Oh! Of "Innocence Extinct"!

Forgotten now…are "stepping stones" once gathered in the march of time While computers conjure-up new ideas…"mortal minds" are now lain aside.

Continue…

Innocence Extinct
"The Last Dinosaur"

Remember times now gone by of happier days seen, when neighborhood playgrounds were filled with dreams…and the young played so innocently. Joy and laughter would abound in games played, and together they were having fun. Many of those playgrounds have now grounded quiet as they lie empty in the "silence of the sun". Today it seems no one plays for fun!

I find now "Innocence Extinct" or so it appears to be, as there is reason in believing the lessons of learning and the "Stepping Stones"…experienced in life's ledger towards manhood, are being replaced…in a world insisting to be comprised in…

"Automated Computerized Machinery".

Too busy are all with videos, games, and gadgets with "personal screens", with heads tilted down and of thumbs and fingers pressing "buttons" and "keys". As they all "play in contact" with no one real nor of anyone seen!

A new world has been created and is being lived and played in a "Sphere" known and seen as…

"Virtual Reality".

As these "stories" unfold within the "tellings" reminiscent of a relic old…I recall when time and age came "a calling too soon", as minds were being "shaped" and futures were being groomed.

And the "Children of Innocence" have since matured…
            …as long ago "Stepping stone's", are not grown anymore.

In eyes not yet faded and in memories not lost too…I stay unchanged by… "The Sands of Time"…standing unstill as **THE LAST DINOSAUR**…to you!

Category Number Eleven

*Impressions: In Wonder...

...Of "The Telling" Eye*

The following pages...

...Provide a blend...

...Of prose and poetry...

...And a final message...in view to life's inner quandary...

The following subjects included are:

The Forgotten Years

Alas! Breathe yon heavy…of thy last gasp
For man's future shall soon be man's past
As the final match in his "Games Of War",
Has been tamped-down…lit and torched.

And thus shall "The Growing Pains Of Life"
Man had thought learned stay forever lost
As object lessons were falsely being taught
With "Terms Of Life" attached…as its cost!

Let then man's demise be…Remembered…

…As…

…"The Forgotten Years"…!

Spitballin'…

As one surrounds themselves in a particular
Environment and decides to languish there…
They become a product of its environment.

Let it be known: I can only give of myself to you…
As much respect as you allow yourself to receive!

When the…"Voice"…of the people band together
There is nothing more powerful nor more potent,
That can initiate "Change" in the common world!

People seem to be moving much too fast and too far
And I wonder if they know what they are doing it for.

A State Of Mind

Let none allow of life's adversity nor of its disappointment to reign supreme. Inevitably…so shall the stain of hatred and its bitterness stay upon you. And as the years takes its toll…not only will it consume you, it will invariably wear you down and thus…so shall you slowly begin to wither away.

J.J.R.

Strength-Measure-Character: are attributes of stature. For when developed, are indicative of goodness and truth. Hold dear those qualities, for each one possesses the genuine articles that are deemed paramount in serving as your touchstone to all!

The Face Of Adversity

A sign of strength is a characteristic brought about, not only by the adversities that may stand to oppose that person, but within how they battle through the constant confrontations and against its continued persistence. In response to the challenges brought on by "The Face Of Adversity", an undaunted strength subsequently strives to maintain sustenance to their will of perseverance….as they fight to negate its effects. So too, does their "mettle" bear its weight into how that person reacts to pressures in overcoming the vehemence of its over--whelming presence.

The Voice Of Virtue

"The Voice Of Virtue"…exhibits valor and prominence to the call: the measure of a person. This particular attribute comes to the forefront when one may be somewhat beleaguered, lost, or simply crestfallen. They emit a certain quality given of authoritativeness that endeavours not to succumb…but rather, belies

Continue…

the need to ascend and compete. For it has been said: "It is not how many times one is knocked down but how many times one gets back up". Thusly as they so display of their intestinal fortitude from within, not only do they elicit an inner consternation, but as well; an earnest and yet stern and self-reliant...conviction of belief...that is undeniably conveyed to all. This mark, and this measure of a person can be characterized as an...."Untelling Tell", into the unyielding steadfastness and unboundless-relent to carry forward.

...Troubled Times...

The word of truth is the source of nourishment that feeds what is termed as the character of a person. Pursuant to this narrative...character comes about not only by adversity and/or its disappointments, but by a patience, that tends to serve merit regarding an understanding of life and its "eerie" underlying manners that all will eventually experience. It is needed to be understood that one must act accordingly as they take into consideration, the reality that "Troubled Times" whether "Telling" or "Untelling" are not theirs alone. When troubled, they exude an awareness eyed during times of unsettling moments of "darkness and despair". The results of decisions made, may be capable in causing undue residual effects not only to them-selves, but...to the many that have been stationed within the inner realms of their circle of existence.

In view of such knowledge and with..quiet solace and learned wisdom...the character, strength, and measure of a person embolden's a commandment of dignity with integrity. Thus do they valiant forth while becoming ever so formidable a foe to the throes' of adversity and of life's disappointments.

The Epilogue

The "Tellings" as written, is a "reveal" into the author's life and in the eyes of his mind's experience. It is an exercise to also *"enlight"* the open mind, of past thoughts, which may have since been kept buried…of the fact that:

"You Are Not Alone"…!

These "Tellings" that have now been read, have also served purpose as an "Overview" into the "Untellings"…of one's odyssey in a life's adventure of a man's dealings and in the handling of his said feelings. It has been solely written and told from a perspective point of view; as recognized in a mind once known as sane, that has since been ravaged by time and change.

You have read of evil and good, its torment and horror, of love's loss, and of the joys and sorrows felt, that all may go through. Tales told in poetic-verse and in prose written reminiscent in memories of "Days of Old", was scripted as another purpose so proposed…for the "Tellings" to be told.

As such, of this odyssey that has been so well-travelled and now seems to be nearing its end, it may be a surprise to all, of the author's "Telling Call".

In recognizing an unstable mind, and in knowing his time is running short, the author has presented to you, his reading audience, his "Lasting Recall" to the many dangers that play into every episode of… "The Tellings"…and "The Untellings" of this world.

So be aware of your journey and in these intrinsic/esoteric *"tellings"* told. For some topics may have been pleasurable while some beneficial. Some hopefully have been valuable and educational, too. Know too, that these stories written may disturb and some hard to bear. Yet, all however, are written…not only to enlighten…but to "Lighten Our Fears"!

IN FINAL SUMMARY

The author in his written work titled "The Tellings" and "The Untellings"…
presents to the readers…selective compositions…applicable, of the many
scenes, happenings, and events, that depict the somewhat unfathomable
experiences that may encompass one's journey through life.

Written with intended purpose are odysseys, saga's, and tales, relative to
life's trials and tribulations. Many episodes have been written somewhat
shortened and concised…into a tome of one-page studies that are stayed
kept and engrained unto the darkest and deepest recesses of one's mind.

Each individual journey, as so written, enlists its readers to thus become…
somewhat curious, somewhat enlightened, and somewhat "heightened",
by the aspects that show…"Sense And Exposure Of Being".

In doing so, the author has put in print a myriad of inferred suggestions to
be hopefully questioned, scrutinized, and thus ferreted out by its readers.
These various categorical excursions written, are seen served as a glimpse
into one's personal and introspective psyche of the analytic mind, as is so
endured and perhaps…so possessed.

Characteristic of lines accented through iambic verse and in prose poetic;
"The Tellings" and "The Untellings" do metaphorically reveal impressions
indicative to one's hidden secrets. Though dormant and unseen at times
One's innermost emotions may lay transparent and exposed. See below:

Read and re-examine "Shades Of shadows" and "The Shattering Mirror".
Give some thought as to its subject matter and content within its filtered
context. Take note of the author's perspectives and intent, within those
written subjects. For…."The Tellings" and "The Untellings"…bear witness
discreetly and indirectly of the above said emotions and thoughts, and in
the handling of one's feelings as they…act and react…in the aftermath of
experiencing, then repressing, the traumatic effects of…"Sexual Abuse".

Know too…the thought-provoking and contemptible contemplations that
are withheld within "The Tellings" and "The Untellings"…; of the tides of
decisions and of the resulting harsh realities that stand besieged by truth.
Moreover, as one carries forth through "The Eyes Of Life's Journey"…and
beyond, into the abysms of an unrecognizable nether world that holds of
"The Subconcious Realm"…only then will one come to eventually realize…

…"They Are Not Alone"!

Of "The Untellings" Told   "The Tellings" Of The Soul

IN SECRET LIE

From The Private Written Files Of The J.R. Trove:

"THE TELLINGS"

Impressions In Essay-Diatribes In Tale-Truths In Beliefs

AND

In Lament Soliloquy Touched In Prose…Versed In Poetry

"THE UNTELLINGS"

**OF A WORLD SEEN THROUGH THE EYES
OF LIFES JOURNEY**

IN SECRET LIE

"THE TELLINGS"

AND

"THE UNTELLINGS"

The journeys of life, of love, of loss, and of its…"trials and tribulations"…
as so encountered by each, whether chosen or have had thrust upon us,
may dictate actions in reactions perhaps reconciliatory of approval within
an appeased approach given of a rationalizing in the moment, of a mind
somewhat awry, framing its way towards the realization of the inevitable.

However, be not so blinded by those notions as they spring forth, for the
inevitable is a reality of fact all must face. Such are the written words of…
"The Tellings" and "The Untellings"…

…YOU ARE NOT ALONE…

CHRONOLOGICAL SKETCHINGS
OF A RECENT HISTORY IN CONFLICT

*"From there to here,
to here and now,
to from now to there"*

-From The Files Of The J.R. Brief-

CHRONOLOGICAL SKETCHINGS
OF A RECENT HISTORY IN CONFLICT

Table of Contents

THE PROLOGUE

Continued writings brought forth within its second half section of this book consists of various excerpts and "out-takes" revised from the author's first intial book. It has purposes as an exercise in political study and of insight into the sequences {in glimpses}, into our recent and current events.

Subject matter will be consistent within the themes of this text as it has also been written with the intention for all to perhaps gain some "light" as to the sequential time-lines and man's **"played"** involvements as such. Included are segments fraught of histories fragmented time-frames that have been ladened and burdened with continued manipulative tactics of deceit in, and of: **"ego, money, power, and greed."**

Narratives have also been written in a style as to plant **"seeds"** to provide **"food for thought"** to you, the readers.

All may come to recognize as this text has been writ, that the author is perhaps conveying to his readers, of a phrase that has substantive conjecture and that its meanings of truism shall not be denied:

"Not all seen is necessarily black or white."

However, let it also be known that what is and has been termed **"gray"**, has many measures created through the formulas given of man's calculations.

Always has there been wars and always has there been conflicts and always has there been a backlash of hatreds against all at one time or another. Always, amazingly so, man has sustained and survived to carry on. Avenues shall open to continue to do so!

As this text carries forth of the theme **"from there to here, to here and now, to from now to there"**, all will possibly have a better understanding of how the latter will be accomplished!

In **"glimpses and sketches of tidbits"**, subject matter as referenced has been brought before you, written and voiced within a conceptualistic vernacular intonated in speculative degrees that perhaps history may record, as all strive for survival towards a 22nd century and beyond.

Chronologic Sketchings of a Recent History in Conflict

...Sectional Out-Takes From The J.R. Brief Files...

During the last half of the 20th century and continuing now through the 21st century and the new millennium, hidden agendas and advances being applied and marshalled through manipulative usages in technological and automated communicative machinations, have scaled heights of deceit not ever imagined nor dreamed of in the "Commonwealth" features designed by our "Founding Fathers" during the developmental beginning stages (phases) of nation building and infrastructure of these "United States of America".

The course of whence began of this highly touted and somewhat willful innovative excursion encapsulating this so-called "New World Order" theme and the subsequent substantiation of its escalating appetizing spread of indulgent dominance, can be attributed to what can best be described as "ego" consistent with the lure and desire "hell bent" of "money, power, and greed". It's "faces" have been presented before.

All have been inclusive of the aspects considered with being inhabited of the "delusional entitlement" concept as recognized of the "me syndrome". Similar signs surfaced as introduced in WWII!

Reflective of the phrase "A History Doomed To Repeating Itself", a repetitive reviving has been opaquely steam-rolling ubiquitously in this evolutionary course of what has been termed as: "Government Red Tape". Its "wrench-like hold" of government control with its hyperbole, "spin", and rhetoric, is being contested and questioned by all. Consequently, this spiraling downward tailspin is now being given voice against its myriad of "Alibi's Of Lies".

The creative advances of our own technological machinations has allowed for communicative modes of public exposure of continued faulted government handling and its widespread network of "sleighted" tactics.

This vainglorious yet vacuous and indeed onerous show of "self-serving government" indicative of the "Me Syndrome", is now un-shed, naked, and unshielded. All of which can now be witnessed by a subtle re-awakening of the masses, via a 24/7 media broadcasting of our, politics, policies, and political discourse; reflective of "these ages", as in this "Here And Now" theme.

Subsequent of these resulting actions continuously being employed by said government leaders and the elitists, we, this nation, have let our guard down by administering to all, an ostentatious *"Chrome Cavalier Attitude"*.

Consequently, an unspoken declaration of this "bravado of superiority" no longer is believed, no longer scares, nor frightens ally and adversary alike! We have in part become "A House Built Of Cards".

The attempt to continue this flow through the years by oh so many, for the "money, power, and greed" ethics in distinctive correlation of the "me syndrome" with the "egos" of the times that be, simply cannot and must not be tolerated!

Continue...

Assuaged by political rhetoric and held hostage with innuendo of "favored entitlements" accepted, a "silent majority" stayed in its fold. With a concerted strategy, manipulative maneuvers became the focal exercise for such actions to be on-going in this self-established "New World Order" of government control with which much practice in "the dormant years" (of our sleep), had been so perfected to a tee.

This now 21st century governing climate began to rely on its own faulted beliefs and in its own superficial hyperbole. Thusly, it decided to attend with false presumptive focus consistent with a criterion agenda, indicative of iconic unabashed egocentric pragmatism in assimilating its "body of control" towards these convoluted "provocateur" mannerisms so designed in deception.

All had continued with the advent of the so-called "information age". Unbeknownst to an American majority which had been in "slumber" were "renewed actions" by "renewed forbearers" that espoused a "renewed unionization" so conjoined with "theory" of a "renewed ideology" proselytizing this "renewed World Order".

The charade impacted "enmasse" of this transfixed styled coma has been subliminal suggestions so mesmerizing in its manners, that it thusly kept: *voices silent, identities lost, and individuality invisible.*
With that loss of hope towards the bonds of uniformity for a structured society, much damage was created causing this vile debauched state of inequities that is now possessing this nation in this "framed timeline" of a new 21st century millennium.

An attempt at control by our leaders, elitists, and "shadowed" think-tank councils, was and had been devised for our so-called prioritized needs and our so-called advantageous usages of this worldwide "phenomenon". Acts committed by such "Councils Of Advisors" have now, on further examination been identified and seen as being somewhat "skewed". Its cause and effect has since expanded in "Diabolic Makeshift" in and of, an "Abhorrent" and "Unconscionable" discourse being steered astray. Today, in controversy, are the exposed inequities coddling an "Iodined Toxic Axiom" being reintroduced within philosophical tonings interpreted and espoused as an … "Ideologue In Conceptualistic Principles"!

The continued diatribes as being voiced still, by our "Social Leaders" and "Government Representatives" and "Political Advisors" proposing its "International World Globalization", and enveloping it with such masked slogans as "An Advanced Shared Society" and the all too familiar "Political Diplomacy", (though) embedded in and of "Political Correctness", have not taken full "ROOT".

Take note: the philosophical overtones of the ideologues as so stated, do have merit and meaning. …WHY THEN HAVE THEY FAILED?...

Reasons as to "Failure Of Fruition" are too numerous to extrapolate in full, at this time. Further in-depth examination will be set forth in the on-going chapters and subject material in these, "THE FILES OF THE J.R. BRIEF". …THERE ARE ANSWERS!...

However, at this time concerning these "CHRONOLOGIC SKETCHINGS" as has been written and read to this point, it is of utmost importance for all to be aware of the following: it has become ever so clear that our political, military, and administrative leaders, could not nor perhaps found they were not able to "exact a full control" implementing their plans due to the "revival" of the "forgotten man" and the challenges brought forward by an ever-fast changing world that they themselves helped create.

Ah! "But For The Best Laid Plans Of Mice And Men!"

Random Sketchings: A Prelude
To a Recent History in Turmoil

Calamitous of its feigned political rhetoric exposed in both 2016 and 2020 campaigns, fraught in and of its very own self-condemnation, has now given notice further of an ensuing under-current belly of (bias) innuendo. As the "machines of man" rifled full disclosures of a "matrix network" shadowed in a series of tunneled mazes wrought in devious tactical actions given of "manipulative deceit"..."True Colors" were now being bared!

While examining these maneuvered decisions despicably performed in subtle nondescript incremental processions planned and parlayed by the "higher powers", one may give pause to reason(s) for this seemingly "semi-self-induced (sub) conscious coma" *that blanketed oh so many during these past fifty plus years.*

As all had complacently let avalanche into a mushroom of political and social-societal disgraces binded with copious acts in display of denigrated decay, all forwarded blindly into foals encumbered within the replicated morass of diseases being flagrantly set anew.

All however can now rise towards a "renewed awakening" of its once past "comatose sleeping giant" ownership. An "umbrella" of "fictitious lies of distortions", of "secret agendas", and "disingenuous false representations" are so now magnified in this "24/7 info-media age", it has brought forth "surface" to all, of our world views.

As such, an acceptance of strength and a respect in power as previously held by the nations of the world have now wavered and is continuing to wane evermore in rapid succession.

An accomplished world now notified in expanded knowledge through electronic new age developments consistent with a w.w.w. networking, interwoven within the technological innovations constantly being revised of, in, and by, the automated "machines of man", have introduced all to the distinct possibility that an "America" as a "super world power" no longer may quite exist, nor wish to exert, nor have the ambition or the means to do so.

The importance for a renewed rededication for man and all of humanities survival to continue on, must make its move now with mandatory drastic changes to stem the ramifications that have and will continue to take hold of this now poisonous culture as has been recognized and identified as a "Malignant Cancer", (untouched)!

Of the opportunity, to wit, that may be afforded to all for a sustainable and perhaps a prosperous future...

...All need take notice of the purposeness in coalescing the many differentiating aspects as has been promulgated by dissertations in "Paradigm Dynamics" in so prerequisitioning the "Synergistic Keys" that may yet still be developed, embraced, and entertained, by an intelligence that shall be reached, and rewarded in its fruition in the furthering of a "Modernization In Civilization" of mankind, now and beyond.

The Rebirth of an America

As many have ladened themselves of indignities with prejudices, and have fallen victims to sins of neglect and spite, and have denigrated themselves with shown signs of complacency complicit with the folly of the "**me syndrome**", all have thus betrayed themselves. It is the loss of the real fires that had burned and yearned, that had given "backbone of strength" and an "indomitable spirit" that had once enabled us in becoming a free people, and a free nation. It hath given rise to the word and to the world: "**Independence**". As in the history records so established as the "**Declaration of Independence**".

Know that words spoken by our Founding Forefathers of "**Life**", "**Liberty**" and the "**Pursuit of Happiness**" has much importance in meaning and exercise. It is simplistic, strong, and to the point. Very straight forward and what is now needed to be understood in full. Once digested, all must attempt to regain these goals and to sense the purposeness of said goals to be accomplished.

So to get from "**here to there**", all must shine that light towards that other end of the tunnel. Continued steps to approach include, if time allows, a serious energy to gradually band together to deconstruct all that has been tattered and shattered, then reconstruct all that can be re-established for remedy. A workforce, independent of itself, and formulated of good will, will in fact not only build infrastructure, and not only build commerce & production, it will build the people and the lands they live and work on. A nation thus strengthened, can behold of the *fruits of fruition* and have witness as to the next rebirth of the previously aforementioned: a "Modernization in Civilization".

Businesses will grow, trades will grow, and funds for the schools, colleges, teachers, doctors, hospitals, and all manufacturers will grow. Such cause and effect will again rebuild a "**backbone**" that had once existed…called: "**Middle Class America**". With strength, all will again enjoy a growth in employment. And a welcomed comeback. As all structure and framework becomes strengthened with solid growth, an "American" nations maturity will come to have a safe-guard within a redeveloped military and in its national security system.

With a new thirst and with a renewed energy and with solid leadership direction, commerce and trade will extend forward as infrastructure redevelops. Banking, economics, intermeshed with employment and production, will increase and gain, and manufacturing, shipping, and international foreign trade equalized for the nations in concerns of imports and exports etc… **will blossom for all**… **only if time allows**.

To ask how, after all these years of so much in-house suffering and turmoil do to aspects of down-turned economical cycles do we dare to now invoke a just proclamation that can now lift us up from these past several decades of doldrums?

Let us try to give "**food for though**t", in contemplation, introspection, and in reflections of history.

Continue…

The Rebirth of an America

Simply put, study and read, then comprehend of the events in history that transpired some 240 years ago. Although there were many obstacles, adversities, and trials of tribulations to overcome at the time, the fight and the dreams for the development of an "Independence" would soon become reality.

And so, a country, a united nation of states, an "**America**", did indeed spring forth. It hath done so with unity in a realized direction given of focus with, once again: a "back-bone" as the "key"!

The right peoples with the right leadership qualities for the right needs, wants, and given of the true hopes for equality within all, can make all happen again.

All, with the proper tools for guidance as once was in use after a WWII, can be substantially "**new and improved**", for remember as has been referenced, all have the benefit of what is termed a "**template**" to work from.

The scheduling of imperative tactical movements as this timeline now forages onward, should be ever so ticketed enroute of the avenues for the causes of: "*Freedom, Independence*", and dear I say "GOD".

The elimination of fear, and the eradication and decimation of terror as has been burrowed through by the machinations of mankind's own blend of terrorism, needs to be now silenced.

As exercises in thoughts and ideas have given of some glimpses for all to move from "**here to there**", it may be quite startling to ingest exactly what may be out "**there**".

Of cause and effect and of scenario's that may exist and of the scenario's that may be formed to exist, may I remind all that a drastic change is and has been needed to take its place in time, now! If not now, it may never.

If change is not executed within the current phase of this "**here and now**" position, what may all to soon transpire will bring cause for all to be alarmed. Hence, such may be a revisit likened to the "**Burning of Rome**" amidst the case in point of "**The Fall of the Roman Empire**".

However, as stated beforehand if time allows, and all aspects prevail, then with proper direction an **America** will again stand tall. A rebirth of a United States will thus be enhanced with titles of previous status-quo given of "**super world power**" and the "**worlds nation builder**".

There is plenty written that can attest to the phraseology termed as "**a history repeating itself**". It may bring study tangent to a WWII facsimile in sequences there of.

Let It Be Known…"Be Careful What You Wish"!

* A Matter of Conjecture *

There is always a rush to judgement as many may differ with the results and the processes leading to said results.

Know that most who question, do so after the fact. That factor is what is generally known to be called as "**hindsight**".

In this text, what has been written is for all to be a bit more aware of the compilating sequential complexities of decision-making of the times and of some of the peoples involved within these recent events of these last several decades in this written theme:

"From there to here, to here and now, to from now to there"

There are degrees of blame to be assigned. As there are many errors of judgement to go around.

However, with full study into the record books, it is for you, the reader, to assess and perhaps speculate as to the reasons and the purposes for all decisions and judgements made along the way.

Know this: Errors in judgement may come about in several baneful manners. As in errors of incompetence and errors of omission which are inexcusable. Errors caused of arrogance, ego, and ignorance are cited as deplorable. Decisions and actions or inactions with known intent of any wrong-doing, are errors of unacceptability. And are horrendously unspeakable.

However, intentional acts of deceit, ever so performed and executed for political greed and power, combined with a deniability…are reprehensible. These are acts… that are cited as **"TREASON"**.

In giving pause, again, as attempts to give some incite to these glimpses of tidbits of info into the processes of some of the varying perspectives that have found their way into the decisions along the very intricate network of timeline events, we find we do have some answers. We also find we still have some questions as yet unanswered.

Always as has been written, history has had common threads and common denominators, such as "ego, power, money, greed", and degrees of "delusional" thinkings', as many were and had been afflicted with "dreams" of world dominance.

However, *"delusions with egocentric tendencies",* may also be fertilized of principles and beliefs with a good will for all. "**The ego and the id**" may be framed for a better world, not a dictatorial one.

In times along this history, all have been driven with the same attitudes, the same decision-making, and the same purposes; to maintain and attain with growth the same results. "**Ego, power, money, and greed**" has a long timeline.

It is quite difficult then, to interject change with a philosophical bent towards a world order that would equalize all nations in the form of a new "**globalized governmental solidarity**". As the "status-quo" would not "*concede*" and the "new age leaders" would not fully "*abandon*"; compromises were needed to be ironed out and newly implemented.

When such is the case, beliefs and morals are put to task. How one deals with such, may be the way one can "**tell**" "the measure of the man".

Understand by all, that what one professes and proceeds to act on, may be viewed and subjected to what is termed "**a telling**". If one has the eyes of the world on them, they need to be proficient at "**guising.**" If so, "**a telling**" may leave all with an unsure "**frame**" of said purposes. However, "**a telling**" can also be made known to all in view by what may not be said and the actions or inactions not performed.

One must have knowledge as to ride this "**slippery slope**" without a "**falling**", and without presenting a verifiable "**tell**" to an enemy. It is a much more serious matter when a nation's national security and safety of its peoples are in jeopardy.

…No More…

Is…"The wool being pulled over anyone's eyes"!

CHRONOLOGICAL SKETCHINGS
OF A RECENT HISTORY IN CONFLICT

* In Final Summary *

There is much "**food for thought**" for all, for a long time. That is, only if time allows to answer all questions asked.

From a cyst, to a tumor, to what has now metastasized into a living breathing cancer.

How much further can all thread?

Indeed, with the threats of weapons of mass destruction and nuclear proliferation being developed and sought by nations that have a common thread, of which is the extreme hatred of the **United States**, an outlook may be bleak.

The continued escalation of war...both internal and external...being carried forth from the 20th century into this 21st century, may give inference of a final accounting of a history not only repeating itself, but quite possibly giving credence to the:

"Bible's Prophecies Of Its Truths".

In the final analysis, in order to save the civilizations of mankind, it is with us to have a clear mind and an honest intention for all to proceed to handle and manage this world that is now turned upside down. It can be achieved!

"As So It Is Written...So Shall It Come To Pass".

About the Author

His genius lies within each line of his verse...within each phrase of his prose.
His madness lies within "The Tellings" of the soul and of "The Untellings" told.

His genius lies within..."The Interpretations"...to so be perceived by one and all.
His madness lies within a "Tapestry of emotions" unseen, untapped, and taboo...
And whether secreted or hidden from view...all are yet known and felt by you!

There is a fine line unseen, though beheld (in twist) of: "Genius and Madness".
"The Tellings" and "The Untellings"...as so written, manages to capture it all...
Combining both: the very concept and its definition of: "Genius-vs-Madness"!

Printed in the United States
By Bookmasters